Urban
Coyote

A Yukon Anthology

Michele Genest and Dianne Homan, Editors

THE YUKON PUBLISHERS
Whitehorse

Published by Lost Moose Publishing 58 Kluane Cres., Whitehorse, Yukon, Canada Y1A 3G7 Phone 867-668-5076 or 668-3441. Fax 867-668-6223. Email lmoose@yknet.ca Web www.lostmoose.net

National Library of Canada cataloguing in publication data

Main entry under title :
Urban Coyote : a Yukon anthology

ISBN 1-896758-07X

1. Yukon Territory — Literary collections. 2. Canadian literature (English) — Yukon Territory. I. Genest, Michele. II. Homan, Dianne

PS8255.Y8U72 2001   C810.8'09719'1   C2001-980266-8

Printed and bound in Canada

Book design and production by Patricia Halladay
Cover photograph by Peter Long

The Urban Coyote Collective and Lost Moose Publishing wish to gratefully acknowledge a contribution from the Government of Yukon, Arts Fund, which made publication of this volume possible.

Future submissions are invited. Contact the Urban Coyote Collective at 710 Strickland Street, Whitehorse, Yukon, Y1A 2K8.

Second Printing, March 2002

Acknowledgements

We would like to thank a few people, without whom this book wouldn't have been possible. Patricia Robertson, who must take credit for being the catalyst. Janet Genest, for her love of the wilderness and her provision of boiled eggs, oranges, and cold, hard cash. Phyllis Homan, for instilling a love of language and its structures.

John Eerkes-Medrano, who teaches by example, for his invaluable contribution in editing the manuscript. Laurel Parry, guide, consultant, and friend, who gave us the book's title. And to all those who encouraged us, submitted work, asked questions, and wondered when on earth the project would be finished, thank you. This book is for you.

Michele Genest
Dianne Homan

Preface

The literature of a region is often redolent with place. As poet Erling Friis-Baastad, one of our contributors, has said about living in the north, "After a while you hear the world a little differently, you see it a little differently, you pass it through a different set of filters. It's very subtle."

In the recent years of the Yukon's history, another subtle change has taken place. Many of us live with one foot in the city or town and the other foot in the wilderness. It was in an attempt to capture the peculiar essence of that experience that we put this anthology together. And what better name, we thought, than Urban Coyote? It is a title that captures, for us, the sense of worlds intersecting — of bush meeting asphalt, of trapline meeting supermarket.

This experience is not unique to the north, but these stories are. As our world changes — and it's changing quickly — we hope we have recorded something of what it is to live here, now, in the wild and in the city, in the voices of our writers and poets.

Michele Genest
Dianne Homan
Whitehorse, Yukon Territory
August 2001

Contents

Introduction

Brian Brett

Some landscapes are identified by great events — heroic battles such as Thermopylae and the Alamo, or large-scale horrors: Auschwitz. Some are marked by massive constructions, like the pyramids of Giza, or natural cataclysms, like the volcanic island of Krakatoa. Others are marked by episodes of astonishing human actions.

The Yukon is such a realm. The shock of the gold rush of '98 forever altered its landscape and its native peoples, and left behind a gold mine of tall tales and stories about the invading gold seekers.

Communities can become so obsessed by their past that they can visualize nothing else. For more than a century the Yukon has bathed in the golden glow of its too often romanticized mad moment in history, along with the glow of its other enduring myth, that it is one of the earth's last frontiers (as wild and fabled as the Amazon) — the wilderness that the world used to be.

During my time in the Yukon I was fortunate enough to witness some of its untamed spirit — it really is an island in a world of crushing development and pollution.

But while I admire the romance of the gold rush, I think I was more possessed by the landscape and the wildlife — the grizzly bears, the moose, the lynx, the wolverine I saw floating like a magic carpet possessed by demons across the ground, the wolf glancing up from a thawing creek with a placid grace and intelligence that made me feel forever the intruder.

But the present can't be ignored — the invasion of the modern age, the changing lives of a community. Too many believe they can dwell in the past forever, or that the wild will remain wild without help. Unfortunately the Yukon, like the Amazon, is no longer truly wild. Celebrities cruise by for a holiday. You can get the best coffee, imported from anywhere in the world, in Whitehorse. Several communities are already governed by the grab-and-ruin mentality which has turned great towns on this continent into ghettoes and strip malls.

That's why the creation of this anthology is an exciting idea, one long overdue. Here's a work that acknowledges both the Yukon's wilderness and its new, urban realities. *Urban Coyote.* The coyote is a graceful, wild animal, but it also has the smarts to survive in the city. It knows how to move between environments, a necessary change for Yukon writers.

Robert Service took doggerel adventures and elevated them to high art. Jack London told some of the most gripping, if occasionally inaccurate, stories to ever come out of the north. But times have changed. The coyote has learned to live on the night streets. Civilization intrudes. We must deal with the present — the tourists, the new hip generation, and the corporate developers, while retaining those great old memories. That's what these authors do, that's where they come from.

We are given the seasons, their power and colour, a sternwheeler in pieces at the bottom of the Yukon River. And a poem that searches for the melting point.

Lisa Guenther's haunting Sauniq captures the interior wilderness where bones and words meet. The loneliness of relationships. Young women and men descending into Whitehorse, a town with a history its city planners are determined to eliminate by imitating the mall-town vision of suburban America, despite the fact most Yukoners are intent on remaining outside of the corporate mould.

There's the sparse elegance of Patricia Robertson's mountain vision, and the mysterious music of Erling Friis-Baastad, two writers whose reputations have spread beyond their home turf.

There are also those classic northern standards like toilet training in winter, and log cabin culture. And the power of the drum, well known since prehistory. The drum isn't leaving. If anything, it's gaining power.

It's a new Yukon, that's for sure. You can sip your cappuccino, nibble fine chocolate desserts, and break great bread, before taking your dog team out for a run. And romance, o yes, romance is everywhere.

Michele Genest goes back to those clay cliffs, rising above Whitehorse, mythic and powerful. Lawrie Crawford updates our e-mail and reads between the lines of modern relationships. Raft builders are just on the edge of town, reaching with their hopes, like the mighty Stan Rogers, for an Arctic sea.

Yvette Nolan charmingly returns us to what we hold in our hands, the written word, how it seeps through the exquisite little town of Atlin, investing everyone with a power given away by one man, the power of books, words.

These urban coyotes know their country, its history and its future. They can be relaxed and resting in their dens or searching for the something that led many to the Yukon. It is, after all, a country of dreaming, and these dreams have taken many forms. Read them, and enjoy the new reality of the Yukon.

The Passage

Jenny Trapnell

When you arrive, you look for the boat. The soft white wood, the hard orange wheel, and the shiny black paint that spells Klondike. And then you see the Yukon River, rushing away with the image you've just touched. It is a long time past, in the present.

It is only later, when you listen to the stories, that you hear the sounds of drums, salmon jumping, and terns calling. You begin to live here deliberately, your life moving like the churn of the boat wheel, like the salmon spawning, like the berries that ripen to the colour of blood each autumn.

There are changes in the land, in how the people here have lived. After twenty years you notice the voices are different. Once a trip to the Sally Ann meant eavesdropping on conversations in Han, or Southern

Tutchone, or something else that seemed more certain than English. Occasionally a word like "zipper" was spoken, as if it were a shiny splash in the river. Then it was gone, into the deep of some place you couldn't know.

At the Edge

At the southern edge of the city is a crescent-shaped subdivision. It is often shadowed by the surrounding escarpment that rims an ancient lake bed. When you look down from the top, you see a caldera. In winter, smoke rises like steam to the heavens. When it clears, you see on the valley bottom two black lines running parallel, connected by giant limbless trees in twenty-metre intervals. They shimmer in the sun, like the wet strands of a web. They form a perimeter, with homes and people on one side and the edge of the wilderness on the other.

Down there is a dirt road and a trail alongside the wires, and when you walk or run it, you can hear the hum of electricity. When it's forty below, the sound conjures up hot showers and dishwashers, and lights that illuminate bedtime stories. But in a second you can veer off and stand in the willow, the pines, and the spruce, and hide and be hidden, where it is dark, and quiet and free.

All year long the wires sing. One winter morning, feet crunching in the cold, I heard a loud and rapid hammer. Woodpeckers, like solitary drill sergeants, were attacking the hydroelectric poles. After one drill ended, another began farther down the line. Duelling woodpeckers. When I followed the beat, I found a black-headed bird with a tuft of red, unaware of my presence, beating its head against the top of the pole. The hole it made was perfectly round.

Fall

After some years, I notice there is a seasonal round here at the edge. Fall brings cranberries in clusters. I am a Delilah running her hands through the hair of a god — finding rubies and garnets. (Pick when the sun is at an angle, at sunset or in the early morning, when the light captures the shiny orbs.) They fall into my hands, and my mouth is left stained, my fingers red.

Winter

In winter the coyotes yip and yowl, and sing an eerie revelry. They congregate to watch the sun come up, in ones or twos or more. As I drive to work, I look up and see that where the sun is just touching the crown of the drumlin a coyote is basking, unconcerned with the red lights or green lights, the school crossing guard just below who says go or stop.

Spring

Hockey tournament time. An early morning ride to the arena takes me past the escarpment where five coyotes sit and wait as the sun meets their black eyes. The image sears; it's like a rock outcrop in the Serengeti, just for moments, as the car turns from one four-lane street onto another, and then disappears. I have no invitation to join them. They just sit in a memory, to visit from time to time. I still look for them on the horizon, in the light, in the early morning. But I know they have gone, now, maybe forever. Too much traffic, too wide roads.

I am like the falcon that perches over the now dead marsh, wondering what has happened to all the ducks. The wetland stubbornly refreshes itself in a sodden summer, but the birds do not return. There is hope that at the edge, they will come back and comfort us, forgive us, and give us reasons again to live at their boundary.

Summer

The holy time. The light will always be with you. The willows scent the air, the animals visit, the skies fill with delicate green birds that sit in the branches for half-seconds and disappear into the budding unfolding leaves, camouflaged, just for fun. Otters play on their backs as they roll down the river. The ice goes, the mud turns to dirt, to dust. You breathe it all in. You know it will heal you.

Boys laugh and leap into the cool river. The sun shines on their bodies like honey. It's easy to get swept away but you know the current. It comes to shore just across from the sternwheeler, in the shallows with the bones.

Thin Ice

Mitch Miyagawa

Two rusted red shapes, like a half-moon and a periscope, poke through the snow and ice, twenty feet from where I stand on shore. These are remnants of a sternwheel hub, still intact below the frozen surface of the Yukon River. In a month, when the ice breaks up, before the mountain snows melt and raise the river, the outline of a hull will emerge around the pieces of metal under a fine mud silt. Mixed with the mud are planks from packing crates and broken skinning boards. Half a rudder lies twenty feet away from the boat, as if tossed there. And somewhere, under the sand and stones and gasping cold water, is a brass plate engraved with the name *Clara Monarch*.

There are tracks all around the two metal shapes. Fox paws, the wing fans of magpies and ravens, the tractor swaths of snowmobiles, all criss-cross and overlap on the snow. I do my own criss-crossing, wandering in and out of the train tracks that follow the shore. I'd go out onto the river, but it's been a warm winter. There are cracks in the ice, and downstream I can see open water.

When that open water spreads and the ice goes away, the trumpeter swans will come. For many years they have rested here on their journey north, pulling reeds with their regal white necks near the wreck of the *Clara Monarch*. People driving by will see them from Quartz Road, which runs within twenty feet of this sloughy patch of the river. Some of the drivers will pull over, ignoring the honking and swearing from vehicles behind them. Some will get out to watch, crossing the busy road cautiously, for this long straight section of road is a temptation to speeders. It's spring, some will say, thinking of bicycles and barbecues and watching the floating swans. Then they will have to hazard the road once more, like the coyotes that still try to reach the river from the cliffs on the other side of downtown Whitehorse.

On the other side of the road, away from the river, are forty acres of barren earth. One fall night a few years ago, bulldozers flattened pine and swamp there. This was the last portion of bush in the city core. Hemmed between two busy roads, an industrial park, and a growing strip of fast-food restaurants, its demise was inevitable. Now there are only a few old poplars and spruce left on the riverbanks in this part of town.

The bulldozers scared the coyotes away from the river and back up the bluff, which used to be the bank of the Yukon River. In time, the river flexed away, leaving the marshy wetland that became Whitehorse. Back then the bluff contained Whitehorse, when it was a town. Now Whitehorse has poured over the bluff in all directions. Now it's a city, in size and in attitude. Cities are big. Cities bustle. Cities have shopping malls, like the one that will be built in this flattened square of dirt.

Like the few old trees left on the banks and the sedge grass on the islands that dot this slow patch of the Yukon, the *Clara Monarch* has been at this bend in the river for a long time. Before her arrival, the Ta'an people of Lake Laberge fished here. Kashx̱oot, son of Mundessa, the Old Man Chief, gutted salmon at a camp on the little island just south of the old steamer, an island now named after him. That was before the dance hall girls, the hucksters, and the riverboats came, following the gold-crazy men who once raced for the Klondike. Now the camp is gone, the fish bones feeding what trees are left. And the *Clara Monarch* lies gutted, rotting here for over ninety years in the slough named after her.

I follow the tracks farther, away from the sound of the traffic. Once I reach the open water I've walked as far as I can go without trespassing. I've entered an industrial area. There are signs threatening prosecution, dogs barking in the distance. Metal drums lie half-buried in melting snow. The king of all metal drums stands alone in another barren, bulldozed patch. Lying on its round side, two storeys high, it looks like a giant can of tuna. I turn around and follow my own footprints back towards the *Clara Monarch*.

She was born in San Francisco, like so many of those gold-crazy men, in 1898. She wasn't built for the north, but north she went on a barge that year. A gang of California cheechakos figured they would make their millions sailing men and their ore sacks, heavy or empty, between the gold fields of the Yukon. The 'Frisco hopefuls were smart enough to know, at least, that it wasn't the miners who made the money; it was those who mined the miners.

The *Clara Monarch* ran the Dawson–Whitehorse route for years but never made her owners rich. By the turn of the century there were dozens of sternwheelers on the Yukon River, all competing for the business of the prospectors who lived by gossip and their noses, following the faintest odour of the big strike. The big one, they whispered to each other in the smoky saloons of Dawson City one winter, was the Tanana River. The whispers turned to rumours that flooded the town. The whole city waited for spring. Once the ice disappeared, boats like the *Clara Monarch* took the gold-seekers as far as the mouth of the Tanana, where it spills into the Yukon, four hundred miles downstream of Dawson. Once up the Tanana, they worked in a frenzy, frantically building camps and cutting firewood before the first snow, only three months away.

The steamer *Rock Island* brought one hundred and thirty men back from Tanana in the spring of 1902 — the ones with enough money to pay the fare. Hundreds more, penniless, scrabbled rafts together out of knotted lumber and logs. A boy from Montana barely old enough to vote had broken through thin ice on the way to a dig. The freezing-cold water and a surgeon's saw took his feet; he rode back on the *Rock Island*, walking the deck on his knees. Other men counted their money, hoping to have enough for the fifty-cent bath at the Pioneer Barbershop when they reached Dawson.

Eugene E. Schmitz was one of the *Clara Monarch*'s original owners, a violinist and occasional orchestra leader who had sailed north on the same barge that carried his new steamer. "Handsome Gene," a smooth talker with a moustache and neatly trimmed goatee, had arrived from San Francisco barely two years earlier. When the *Clara Monarch* failed to make him a rich man, or even a man able to pay his bills, he fell back on music and fiddled in dance halls in Dawson and Nome before falling further back to San Francisco.

Back in 'Frisco he had more success. He became the president of the Musicians' Union when the Union Labour Party was at its peak. As a musician, Schmitz was also a part of high society, the perfect candidate for Mayor. He won the civic election of 1901. Handsome Gene — Mayor

Handsome Gene — was still after the easy money he sought in the Klondike. In his years of power, he took bribe after bribe — from Pacific Gas and Electric for their rate hikes, from Home Telephone for a monopoly, from United Railroad to install the overhead trolley system that every San Franciscan hated.

On the eve of the Great Earthquake of 1906, the trolley issue was about to go to a vote. But instead of voting, San Franciscans spent a week fighting the fires that burned half their city. Lucky for Handsome Gene. He escaped the law until the next year, when he was convicted on twenty-seven counts of graft and bribery.

I hear a big truck rumble by on Quartz Road. The ground shakes. When the truck is gone the ice creaks and cracks around the *Clara Monarch*. Somewhere below me, deep inside the earth, rocks are grinding against each other. Last year an earthquake along the Denali Fault, 150 kilometres to the west, rattled coffee cups here. More than two hundred earthquakes a year occur in the Yukon, most too small to be felt.

The *Clara Monarch* never warrants more than a few sentences in books on sternwheelers or Klondike registries. But these few sentences always include mention of her captain, Alexander McLean. No other record of McLean — no newspaper stories, no pictures, no diaries — seem to exist. An Alex McLean was registered with the British Yukon Navigation Company in the

1920s, but there's no indication whether this is the same man. Regardless, he will always be remembered as the inspiration for one of Jack London's most famous characters: Wolf Larsen, the Sea-Wolf.

In 1898, Jack London made the same voyage as Handsome Gene up the west coast to the Alaskan port of Dyea. He climbed the famous Chilkoot Pass with his ton of goods, looking for adventure and that lucky strike. London might have met Alex McLean on his trip to Dawson along the Yukon River. Or he might have just heard stories of McLean, passed to him by miners and sailors. Or maybe McLean himself started a rumour — "You ever read that book by Jack London? That's me in there!" Stories like that are worth grub, after all. Rumours have a way of solidifying and becoming a thin crust over the truth for those who want to believe.

I have my doubts about the connection. If Alexander McLean was anything like London's character, biographies would have been written about him. In London's novel *The Sea-Wolf*, Wolf Larsen — the character London supposedly based on McLean — is the captain of a sealing schooner named *Ghost*. Larsen kills one of his crew with his bare hands, feeling no remorse, only disgust at the rest: "They move; so does the jellyfish move. They move in order to eat in order that they may keep moving … It's a circle; you get nowhere. Neither do they." Larsen summarizes his view: "Life," he says, "is yeasty crawling."

But Jack London never stopped here in Whitehorse.

Like so many Stampeders, he rushed past where I now stand across from the skeleton of the *Clara Monarch*. Yet once Jack London's name became gold, a rumour started that he had spent a summer piloting boats through the foaming rapids from which this city derives its name, just a mile upstream from here.

Rumours and stories still carry the whiff of riches. A few years ago some of the city's boosters proposed naming a local road after Jack London, based on the legend. They dreamt of tourists snapping pictures by the signs, taking a break from their rush to Alaska, maybe spending a few more dollars here. A local historian, the son of a pioneer, proved Jack London's connection to the city was untrue. Local First Nations called London a racist. So the name Two Mile Hill remains, boring and unprofitable, much to the chagrin of some. A missed opportunity, some think, to promise tourists a more colourful past.

I stand by the *Clara Monarch*'s remains again and look across the old steamer to the trees along the bank near Kishwoot Island. City Council plans another road right up against those trees, a big city road fifteen seconds long, at a cost of a hundred thousand dollars a second. It will angle towards Quartz Road and link up with it at the planned entrance to the mall.

Civic dreams have meant concrete and asphalt for a long time here. Before Whitehorse was a city, the townsfolk hungered for roads. "There is not today in the whole of Canada a more promising section than the Yukon," pronounced the *Whitehorse Star* in 1906, "nor is there a section where roads are more needed." Now the Big Road, the Alaska Highway, is a tourist attraction in itself — a part, it is claimed, of engineering history.

It's roads and tourists now, not boats and gold, but the prospectors are still here. They prospect the roads like others did the rivers a hundred years ago, trying to catch tourist dollars. Along the Big Road they've built a museum full of mastodons and sabre-toothed tigers, a multimillion-dollar laser simulation of the northern lights. Along that Big Road there's the world's biggest tribute to roads — a maze of thousands of street and highway signs lined up on posts, started by lonely U.S. Army engineers pushing the road through in World War II. Winter snow in the Sign Post Forest sits on branches of Wichita, Kansas and Gimli, Manitoba.

The boats are almost gone. The *S.S. Klondike* still sits intact by the Yukon River, across town from the *Clara Monarch* — a tourist attraction. But all the others are rusted, drowned relics like the *Clara Monarch*, or sacrificed to progress, or destroyed for no reason at all. The *Canadian* was buried under tons of rock for a road upriver from Whitehorse. The *Tutshi* and the *Casca* were burnt to the ground. The *F.H. Kilbourne* was "cleaned up" and packed to the dump.

When the sternwheelers moved and served a

purpose, they were bought, sold, cut open, made faster, bigger, more comfortable, to try to keep up with the times. The *Clara Monarch* is really half one boat and half another. In 1901, two sets of owners cooperated, taking the machinery and furniture from the *Clara* and putting it into the barge the *Monarch*. But then men fought over her like murderous suitors, for combining the two boats had been an attempt by both owners to escape their debts. By May of 1902, five sets of plaintiffs were trying to pull money from each other like planks from her hull, claiming to have liens and IOUs and salvage rights and injunctions. While they squabbled, the *Clara Monarch* sat abandoned on a sand bar in the river, chunks of ice from the May break-up battering her that spring. The case was settled, but soon the *Clara Monarch* was permanently abandoned.

By 1907, the Rush had died and Dawson was a hollow hull of a once-thriving city. The 'Friscans went back home calling themselves sourdoughs. The *Clara Monarch* died with the Rush, her boilers removed to another steamer, the *Tana*.

The yeasty crawling. In San Francisco, Handsome Gene appealed his case to the California State Supreme Court and was acquitted. He was elected to the Board of Supervisors of San Francisco in 1919. Jack London died of kidney failure before he was forty; some say he killed himself. Wolf Larsen was stranded in his boat, his body gripped by seizures that froze his body but left his mind untouched. A boy with no feet went back home to his parents and got a job cleaning horse's hooves. Told his sourdough stories over and over to a horse's ass.

Our malls push over forests. Our houses are built on swamps. We drive the Big Road. We walk over thin ice.

Towns turn into cities. In this city coyotes still come down from the cliffs, wandering dazed across drive-throughs and parking lots. Ravens still play along the cliffs, catching updrafts, swooping down upon the town to gurgle over toppled garbage cans.

Cities turn into bigger cities. But cities rise and then are smashed in a day by a ripple in the earth. Roads are twisted like licorice. Malls and city halls crumble to the ground. Fires burn houses and bring out flowers. Train tracks are covered with grass. Boats sink into mud and are forgotten. River ice breaks up. And cold, clear water flows, carrying flakes of gold to fools.

Jenny Trapnell was born and raised in Halifax. Trained in journalism, she moved to the Yukon in 1980. She lives in Whitehorse with her husband and two teenage sons.

Mitch Miyagawa lives in Whitehorse. His first play, *The Plum Tree*, will be produced in spring 2002 by Nakai Theatre. He works as an ESL teacher and community development consultant.

The Drummer

Al Pope

A slow steady bass thrum disturbs the chill air of a May morning. At the bottom of Sixth Avenue, the floors of the grey apartments vibrate. A summer student stirs in her sleep when the cotton sheets reverberate against the peach-downed skin of her back. An old woman curled up in her clothes on the riverbank dreams of a long-ago drummer, muscles like tree-burls on his naked shoulders. The first carpenter of the morning stretches his back and remembers a girl, ponytail flapping to the beat of the Jitterbug, chubby hands sweating in his. In a crooked bedroom at the bottom of the clay cliffs, Abe turns over and rests his hand on Sky's waist. She sighs and moves back against him, and her skin is warm where it touches his. He kisses the shadow behind the curve of her chin and whispers.

"You're awake."

The grass at Rotary Park shines with dew that's all but frost. On Second Avenue, commuters squeeze their brakes and peer out through fogged-up windows at the apparition in front of the bandstand. Perched on its tripod of pine poles, the drum looks eight feet tall. The skin could be the whole hide of a good-sized moose. In front of it stands the drummer, a lank, ragged kid in buckskins and beads. He winds up like a baseball player, swings like he's going to drive that poplar stick right through the centre of the drum, but then at the last instant he hesitates. Although two pedestrians on the sidewalk sixty feet away would swear the stick never touches the skin, it sounds.

Two hairs in the mole on Sky's shoulder resonate to the strange booming. Abe is certain she's feigning sleep. He lifts aside the sheet and rises to his hands and knees and then, bending, kisses her waist. He moves down the line of her hip, down her thigh, blowing a thin, tickling draft of breath on her skin, and pauses to kiss the outside of her knee. Drawing a tiny circle with the tip of his tongue on this known sweet spot, he watches for a reaction. Her body tenses, almost imperceptibly. He laughs.

As he repositions himself to tickle the hollow of her spine with his wisp of beard, the rhythm of the drum begins, very gradually, to pick up. From one beat in four seconds to one in three, two, one.

A green '67 Chev pickup, step-side, pulls up to the pumps at Whitehorse Esso. A balding man in work boots gets out and slams the door, scowling toward the park. The gas jockey is a smooth-faced kid; he follows the man's look and laughs.

"What's goin' on down there?"

"Fuck," says the man in work boots. "Fuckin' hippies."

To the editor of the Whitehorse Star, *dear sir I don't know a single real Yukonner thats sat on the bench in front of the post office all summer. Nobody uses it anymore but hippies and drunks. Might as well get rid of it so decent Yukonners can walk the streets safe without having to see that kind of garbage, and get rid of the drummer too so people can here themselves think. A conserned citizen.*

He'll drum for hours, the beat getting gradually faster and then slower again, the simple rhythm never varying. He keeps it up each day until the Mounties come and make him stop because it's late and people are complaining. No one knows why they don't shut him down for good. No one knows why his drum hasn't been vandalized by some sleep-deprived night-shift janitor, or why he hasn't been beaten up by one of the construction workers on the new YTG building. At first, when the drum stops, the whole town sighs with relief, but then after a while there's a sense of something missing.

People stop what they're doing and wonder what's wrong, as if they'd been wearing a hair shirt all their lives and can't get used to not itching. When it starts again there's a moment — just a moment, mind — of relief, before everyone stops what they're doing and raises their eyebrows.

"Oh shit," someone will say. "It's the goddamn drummer again."

In the blue war-built shack along the edge of the clay cliffs, Abe kicks off his shoes and feels the vibration in the floor; bu-ung, says the drum a mile away, and u-ung the worn-out wooden flooring replies. Deep in the earth the sound resonates, growing weaker as it radiates out, but never, never, quite dying.

Yukon, it says, to an SFU English major, waitressing in a truck stop outside of Prince George. What the hell am I doing here? She thinks. There's eight men to every woman in Dawson. Think of the tips. Yukon, it says to a sleeping biker on a broken couch in a Calgary basement hideout. He wakes to an idea: a job in the mines, a new identity. The Yukon, he thinks, nobody'll find me there. Yukon, it says to a scattered world of left-over hippies, new-wave drifters, back-to-the-landers, fugitives and misfits, come to the Yukon. Yes, Abe says, yes, come to the Yukon, kick the doors open, bust the windows, let the winds howl through the place. We're due for an invasion. It's over eighty years since the gold rush, forty since the highway; the place is ready for a change of character. Whitehorse still looks like a gold-rush town with an army camp plastered over it, and it feels like nothing new's happened in — well, at least in Abe's lifetime.

It's funny how the drum disappears after a while, and then all of a sudden you notice it again. Boom, boom, boom. It's begun to spread, too. All over town, the gravel back roads echo to the sound of basement drummers: hip young French Canadians with congas they brought from Africa, heroin addicts drumming their way back from the edge of disaster on rawhide drums their grannies helped them make, skinny high-school kids with lank hair and Sears drum-kits, loose-breasted hippie girls on drums they made themselves out of hollow spruce logs. Car salesmen with pens on desktops.

Some of them riff along, improvising to the beat, others are content to follow the steady bung, bung, bung. Some of them chant or sing or moan along. A few people have begun to pick up the beat on dusty guitars, on pianos out of tune after a hard winter by a wood stove, and clarinets gone slack-valved from lack of use. An old man stands outside the door of his cabin near Ear Lake and scratches a tune on a fiddle he thought he'd given up on thirty years ago.

Each day the hypnotic rhythm seeps deeper into the soul of the town. Pedestrians walk in time to it, a slow, swinging, long-legged stride. Bank clerks count out money to it, cabbies tap it on their steering wheels. The cops who come periodically to shut the drummer down find themselves speaking in time with the drum. Yesterday, an impromptu band gathered in front of the post office. Everything they played, no matter what its metre, rhythm, or tempo, they fit in around the beat of the drum. Their open instrument cases filled up with money so fast it was spilling out onto the street. Hippies opened the gate on the post office lawn and danced barefoot around the mountain ash tree, postal workers inside tapped their feet and wiggled their hips while they sorted the mail. More and more, every day, the town vibrates to the beat of one drum.

When the clay cliff comes through the wall of Abe's house, he's busy trying to tune his guitar. Spatulate fingers as fat and swollen as if all the evening's wine had pooled in the tips grapple with the extreme proximity of the A-string to the D, of D to G. Ears like bags of wet cotton wool struggle with tiny pulses in the ringing harmonics — is that flat, or sharp? He has achieved satisfaction in all but the matter of the ever-awkward B when he's shaken into consciousness of external things by a sound very much like the City of Whitehorse dumptruck turning around in the driveway — except louder, a deep rumble that shakes the house and is followed almost immediately by a thundering boom, the complete collapse of the back wall, and the entry by force of approximately one-third of a houseful of grey-white clay.

"Holy," Abe says.

Ice

Jenny Charchun

That first winter in the north I worked
in a pink diner as a server, my hair in knots,
pulled up in a bun I could barely manage.
I walked to work, five days a week, the same route.
Wrapped until I couldn't recognize myself,
pausing at my reflection in the lobby window
at 5:30 a.m. I swear I was the only human
in that frigid world, my trailing footsteps in fresh snow
temporary evidence of my existence.

In twenty minutes I would be on the bridge,
my cheeks and nose slick with frost,
my scarf moist and unpleasant over my mouth.
I would pause under the reflection of streetlights,
the snow dusting the small cracked mirrors of sidewalk,

like talcum I could spread across my skin to make it
  shine.
The black river moving under my feet,
moving like my pulse, the random chunks of ice the
  reason
for my lethargy, my unwillingness to abandon the world.
I was frozen, my blood thick, unable to gather me,
to align my legs for the steps up and over.

There was too much meaning to those mornings,
that light that's almost there, you know, you can feel it
and you lean into it, trusting.
I would lean over the railing, watching that ice
like parts of me. Gasping at its intentional beauty,
its deliberate size, its calculated movement.
I understand now that it would not have mattered if I
  leaned
until I tumbled like a ball of snow into that blackness of
  myself.
I would have simply floated through my veins, toured my
  body
until I found my heart, the one warmth of that world.
I would have thrown myself bodily onto that fire,
anticipating the ecstasy of melting.

Sauniq

Lisa Guenther

i.

I've got an eye for bones
      skulls and vertebrae
      the sturdy haunch the elegant wing of a pelvis.

I find them
      spilling out of garbage bags
      lying in the forest on a mound of moss.

There: quiet
like a symbol with its meaning rubbed out.

They glow,
like mushrooms in the spring
    : a thigh bone peeling in the river

a porkchop
a bird's beak, almost violet.

I used to collect them. Used to
hang them from the ceiling with wire, put them
on the windowsill, on bookshelves, in pretty Chinese
boxes.
But now I think   maybe

bones belong where you find them.

ii.

There's a word I am learning to say.

Sauniq   (Inuktitut)

    (n.) 1. Bone; 2. Namesake.

We share the same name : we are built of the same
bone

I hold this word   *sauniq*

in my mouth, patiently

waiting for it to melt

like snow upon my tongue

like springtime.

iii.

We walk along the river,
eyes on the ground.

We are looking
for cracks in the ice, we are looking
for something with colour

with smell, something that digs into mud
and pebbles and sticks.

But the river is white. The sky is white.
Our breath is white between us.

Step out of the wind
and cold
Put your hand in my pocket,

and tell me your name

        porous like marrow

your name

        makes room for my own.

Al Pope's fiction and poetry have appeared in *The New Quarterly, The Antigonish Review, Out of Service*, and *Up From The Permafrost*. His radio play *Sunrise in Carcross* was produced on CBC2's *Summer Showcase*, and again on *Out Front*. Four of his short stories have been produced by CBC Radio for *Richardson's Roundup*. His column, "Nordicity," appears weekly in the *Yukon News*.

Born and raised in rural Alberta, **Jenny Charchun** has lived in Whitehorse for six years. She resides downtown, in the purple cabin near the clay cliffs. Her poetry has been published in *Room of One's Own, dig, The Gaspereau Review, CV2*, and *paperplates*.

Lisa Guenther studies and teaches philosophy. She has published poems in *Out of Service* and *The Mitre*.

Two Cups, Two Bowls

Lisa Guenther

We sit in little spaces
     stuffed with moss and fibreglass
held together with chicken wire and bits of string

Spaces padded round with footprints: yours,
mine, the dog's
     footprints of the mouse who crawls in through the
     wall
     and of those invisible creatures
who leave behind as proofs of their existence
small bits of fur, feathers torn from a wing
a corkscrew of shit studded with rosehip seeds

Inside,
we stoke the fire, put the kettle on for tea
wind blowing snow from the roof
jam and pancakes for supper

    the occasional visitor

And we share this open secret:
    that we dwell in little spaces
feet tucked up from the plywood floor
    dreaming of woolly cupboard drawers and knitting
    baskets and
the smooth-worn hollow of old bones

Burrow in deeper: the lichen biting into its stone
    the tongue with its poetry
the rust hooking into the door hinges

You fix the pot of tea and we'll sit here quietly

observing
the distance between raindrops
between swallows who never collide
between the word you said and the word you catch
your breath to say:
window.   raindrop.   star.

Canyon Mountain

Michael Reynolds

When Margaret reaches the radio tower at eight o'clock the sun is still quite high. There's no one else around, so she squats to pee right on the road beside the tower. She doesn't have anything to wipe herself with; she just stays there with her knees in her armpits, letting the wind blow between her legs. The cramp under her ribs is easing and she begins to breathe slower and more deeply. It's the warmest day yet this year.

The road ends here, at the top of this ridge, where the tower and a few small buildings are surrounded by a high fence with three rows of barbed wire strung around the top, like a prison compound. One of the buildings inside the fence has a sign on the door, posted by Northwestel: *Danger. Do Not Enter.* Beyond the fence, the tower itself is enclosed in a second cage.

Criss-cross. The phrase appears in Margaret's mind, a word that forms an X. Like the words *Do Not* on the sign. The dull steel weave of the cage is designed to stop climbers. The diamond-shaped spaces through which she would curl her fingers to pull herself up are sharp-edged and narrow. The edges would pinch her fingers and cut into the bone of her knuckles. The false word *impenetrable* occurs to Margaret. She thinks of tools: *Wirecutters. Hacksaw.*

Margaret is not afraid of the tower, a fact which both surprises and disappoints her. The tower is so simple, and it seems more absurd than powerful now that she's reached it. The ending she had come to begins to retreat again; like a pendulum released from its momentary pause, she feels the renewed momentum of panic.

Over the ridge, at the base of the next mountain, she sees a lake. The sun slides down the spruce-green valley all the way to the water, where particles of silt wink back as from a tropical sea.

Water. On the way up the road, she had been oblivious to her thirst. She kept looking back to town. How it was getting so small. How easily the river moved by it. How low in the valley the town sat. Now she longs only for a drink. *Some water in a clear blue bottle.*

Margaret feels in her pocket where she put the Snickers bar she bought in town hours ago. She had walked off the street and into the store without thinking — out of an urge for destination — but hadn't found anything she wanted to buy. She'd grabbed a chocolate bar, and after paying for it walked back out onto the street, the warm candy clutched awkwardly in her fist like a dead animal. The slight weight of a memory — how, as a three-year-old, she had squeezed the life from the family pet, a gerbil she'd never been allowed to hold. *It might get away.* Standing, the memory of the gerbil swimming in her guts, she'd fixed her gaze on the radio tower, like a giant totem or gallows atop Canyon Mountain.

The wind is cool on the back of her neck, under her hair where her shirt is damp. She licks her finger, wipes a line of salt from her forehead, and licks her finger again. There is no trail, just a series of animal paths that intersect and peter out. Bare hollows beside hummocks of willow. The spruces are spare at the top of the ridge, and grow tight against rock, as if it is these boulders, and not the vein of soil at their base, that have anchored the trees. The trees seem to get thicker all the way down to the lake, where it is all green. She alternately assures and discourages herself about how far it is. She knows that distances appear strange from mountains — too easy, or impossibly far.

Where there are no trees, the ground is covered in a crunchy moss or lichen — deceptively thick, and Margaret walks clumsily, unsure how far she will sink before the ground pushes back on her foot. Every step in the moss releases a perfume like the citronella candles they used to burn at the picnic table on Canada Day, to keep the mosquitoes away.

At night they would have a bonfire, and fireworks. Carla Kostecki and Margaret would run around the yard waving sparklers, transforming the air into a page of evanescent messages, burning their names onto the sky. Already darkness in summer begins to seem exotic to Margaret.

The radio tower is visible only occasionally when she looks back. She should be able to see it from the lake, but between here and that pool she knows she'll be submerged in trees, and neither the tower nor the lake will be in sight.

Margaret notices she is counting forward with each heavy breath: seven months. February. Winter's deepest fold, February is a hazard month, but it stirs in Margaret a fresh surge of defiance, an unlikely thaw. She looks at these trees, so remote from roads and the blades of woodcutters, great round trunks swollen with summer. In February Margaret will be deep in her body and these trees will be here, cradled in the pure weight of snow.

She can't remember a time when she was this alone. She remembers last summer, travelling to Whitehorse on the Greyhound, knowing no one. Listening to the conversations as they stretched across Lake Superior. The voices thinning into prairie darkness. The dream-mingled talk and sick fluorescent light of every

24-hour convenience. Breaking into the scraggly north of B.C. and mounting that last highway in Dawson Creek. Silently changing her mind at every landmark, between every uncomfortable snatch of sleep, until there was no more sleep, no more darkness, just interminable daylight filling her up like caffeine through the winding mountains and jittering her into a tedious sunset and half dusk.

The bus pulled into Whitehorse at four-thirty that morning, the sun already risen behind an overcast sky. The bus station was at the far end of town, across from the Tim Hortons, and everything seemed flat and grey — the mountains a cardboard backdrop propped up behind the town. The bus driver announced that the doughnut shop was the only thing open, and excepting the few people who were met by friends at the station, the whole busload dragged their packs and suitcases across the road and sat down for a final cup of coffee, waiting for the town to come alive.

She met Jay that summer. She got a job waiting tables at the diner in the Family Hotel, and he guided tourists through the *S.S. Klondike* — the big white paddlewheeler that greeted visitors at the bottom of the South Access. This was Jay's second summer, and he was forever talking about what it would be like in the winter. He'd decided to stay. Margaret had no plans to leave either. But Jay's friends were bound for school or travel, and enjoyed this game, telling Jay he was crazy or that they'd send him a postcard from Bangkok. They'd stay till last call at the bars, and then burst out onto the street. Jay and Margaret would walk home in the blur of light between dusk and dawn to Jay's empty apartment in Riverdale.

They'd find a better place to live in the fall, Jay said. They bought a couple of lumpy chairs at a garage sale and a second-hand futon out of the classifieds.

When the sun began to set properly again and the first stars of autumn appeared, Margaret found herself unprepared. Watching the last stars of Orion come to life with the dying August, she realized what had been there all along, the patterns of her life spread out coldly behind the sun.

She did nothing when Jay's friends — her only friends — disappeared one by one. When Jay's inevitable layoff came, shortly after Labour Day. When he came home annoyed that the archives job he'd been counting on had gone to someone who had *completed* their BA, but had only *one* summer of experience. She observed blankly that Jay did nothing. He didn't look for other work. He didn't look for a better place to live. And Margaret did nothing. She thought about how little Jay knew of her. How she had imagined telling him everything this winter. How she would have gotten to know him.

Jay left as the winter's first snowfall arrived in Whitehorse. He told her to wait for him. Why was he pretending that it mattered? Margaret was angry because it didn't matter. She wouldn't walk him to the bus station. She stayed in bed while he flew south on a Greyhound to Vancouver.

Even the locals complained that it was the coldest winter in twenty years. What began as a cold snap stretched into three weeks of forty below.

Margaret's shift at the diner began before buses started running. She'd rise heavily in the pitch dark and wrap herself up double from head to toe. As she left her apartment, the sound of her boots in the hall was a muffled pulse she listened for, beyond her woollen shell. She pushed out of the lobby into the ice fog. Mornings were always a struggle, but there was comfort in the space and privacy of that hour: the thin cushion of warmth that Margaret carried with her every day as she walked across the bridge and through town to work.

Walking the back of this mountain — this isn't loneliness. Loneliness was what Margaret had felt on the Greyhound bus, was how the apartment always felt. This is just being alone — alone in her own thoughts and senses. Her thirst or the sound of her footfalls, like the cold hard air on the bridge of her nose on those mornings walking to work.

Neither is this walk, as Margaret had imagined, all downhill. As she pulls herself up by the roots of a tree and scurries over a lip of rock, she forms a cross-section view of the mountain in her mind. A series of ridges like wrinkles in a balled-up quilt. She can't pause for long. It's only seconds before the blackflies swarm around her head. She can see across to the next ridge, and she knows the lake is somewhere past there.

Water. Margaret remembers a fall trip in grade four to a field centre on the Niagara escarpment. The class played a survival game, each child a designated animal. Carla Kostecki had been a fox, and Margaret a mouse. They all ran around in the woods, looking for tags that represented food and water, and avoiding animals that were above them in the food chain. The herbivores, like Margaret, were at the bottom of the chain. They had to avoid the omnivores and carnivores, or give up their food and water tags and go back to the field centre building.

Margaret had found enough food and water tags for the whole game and was hiding behind a clump of tall grass against a stump. Her knees and elbows were damp from the cold ground, and she had a chill. She was shivering as she watched Jason Sketchley — who was a badger but had wanted to be a wolf — run past her without even slowing down.

When she saw Carla, Carla was already watching her with fox eyes. Margaret froze, and for a moment felt her heart beat wildly. Then Carla put her finger to her lips and silently moved over to Margaret. Without speaking, she began pulling grass and laying it down beside the stump. Margaret did the same. They worked as efficiently as wild animals, crouched on their hands and knees gathering grasses, falling still whenever another sound was heard nearby. When they were satisfied with their nest, the girls lay together and held each other to keep warm. Margaret remembers how she kept her lips pressed firmly together but couldn't help smiling, wanting to stay there forever, waiting for the whistle to call them back in.

When the cold snap finally broke, Margaret stopped going to the diner. She didn't answer the phone when it rang, and on the second day she missed work, her boss came to her apartment and knocked on the door. She hid under the covers. Later that day she phoned and told him she couldn't work anymore.

In grade nine, Margaret and Carla had gone to different high schools. Margaret went to an *enhanced* high school because all her teachers had told her she showed such *promise*. Carla had asked her if she wanted to go there, and for some reason that Margaret still doesn't understand, she had said, *yes*. After that, all Margaret's words took on the uneasy quality of that *yes*, and nothing she said to Carla ever sounded quite right again.

Margaret had gone to university on a full scholarship. In second year, when she was home for reading week, she ran into Mrs. Kostecki, grocery shopping. Carla had gotten married the previous summer and was five months pregnant. *Carla would love to see you*, Mrs.

Kostecki had said. Margaret smiled uneasily. The thought of seeing Carla made her nearly sick with panic. When she got home from the grocery store, she wept.

She had enrolled in a master's program in English literature, with the encouragement of one of her professors. But Margaret was beginning to feel as if she had been tricked into all this schooling. She was good at it — in fact it was effortless — but she didn't feel committed to it. It occurred to Margaret that she couldn't remember the last time she'd made an inspired decision about anything.

She began to let things slide, deliberately missing lectures and ignoring her papers. She felt empowered by her carelessness. She would go to the library or take a walk around campus, strangely hoping to run into one of her professors. And on those occasions when she did, she would make a grand escape — into an elevator, or a thicket of trees, giddy with adrenaline. A concerned professor finally phoned her and suggested that she *take some time off, consider seeing a counsellor.* Margaret had known that her behaviour was becoming alarming. She had wanted there to be no turning back.

Margaret held her breath and dialled. She still knew the Kosteckis' number by heart, though she hadn't phoned Carla in ten years. Of course Carla didn't live there any more, but still when Mrs. Kostecki answered, Margaret knew there was something wrong. She panicked and nearly hung up, then just listened to the pause and the quiet of the Kosteckis' kitchen that carried over the line. *Hello,* Mrs. Kostecki repeated. *Carla, is that you?* Margaret could barely form a voice, but after another pause managed, *Mrs. Kostecki, this is Margaret Evans.*

They both had difficulty speaking, but it was the closest Margaret had felt to anyone in years. Carla had been in a car accident that past summer with her husband and their two-year-old son. Carla and her husband had survived, but their son had died in the accident. They'd moved to a cabin north of Huntsville and didn't have a telephone. It was a hard time, Mrs. Kostecki had said, Carla wasn't speaking to anyone yet.

Margaret bought her Greyhound ticket for White-horse at the end of that month. One of her classmates, she remembered, had spent summers in the Yukon — lots of seasonal work, he said.

After quitting the diner, Margaret did nothing but read, eat, and sleep for nearly three weeks. She hadn't read a book since leaving university, and now books were like candy to her.

In contrast to the cold snap earlier in the winter, February dawned unnaturally warm, and there was considerable thawing. Dull brown grass poked through the snow along the roadside.

Then, in a feathery snowfall that seemed out of place in February, Margaret left the apartment and walked downtown. Nothing stayed. The huge snowflakes disappeared the moment they touched the wet sidewalk. Margaret's hair and cheeks were damp from the flakes that had rested there. At the Sally Ann, she bought a knitted wool toque and took a pair of leather hiking boots, leaving her wet shoes in their place.

After the better part of a year in town she could still sit, anonymous, drinking coffee at the Talisman — a fact that usually upset her. But on this day it made her feel powerful, like the unseen narrator of every life she crossed.

She took the phone number of a cabin for rent downtown, called the landlord from the coffee shop, and saw the place that afternoon. She let her month's rent go on the apartment and started moving into the cabin the next day.

She got a job waiting tables at the Talisman and quickly remembered the unuttered curses that come with all service jobs. She started sleeping with a dish-washer from work. Marc was eighteen, Québécois. His dark hair came down to his chin, where it was sharply cut. He was skittish, had narrow shoulders and a tiny bum, and his English was only slightly better than Margaret's French.

They were more smouldering than in love, each drawn to the strangeness of the other's language and accent, and the taboo of a seven-year age difference. When they were at work, they didn't speak to one another.

The temperature dropped again, but it wouldn't last. The days were getting longer. In the evenings after work, Margaret would hear a knock at her door. This would be Marc, in his thin jacket and wool mitts. She would lead him to the wood stove where he could warm his hands, and the frost would melt from his eyelashes and sparse beard. The cold air that clung to his clothes gave Margaret goosebumps as she undressed, first herself, then him.

Marc had left a month ago to work in Dawson for the summer. Margaret did not mourn his leaving. They had both become less interested in the ritual of Marc's visits, and his going to Dawson gave closure where otherwise they might have lingered too long. When Marc left, he said only, *Goodbye Marguerite.* It had pleased her from the start the way he brought the second syllable of her name to life.

She didn't try to contact Marc when her period was late. It was summer now, and she was sure that she was already in his past. That was fine; she only wondered, vaguely, what kind of a man he would be in five years. Leaving the doctor's office this afternoon, into the oblivious sunlight, she could think of nothing to do but walk. At first, she had felt tricked again, as if her life had been once more given over to someone else's control. And then the weight of her options had made her want to surrender control. And then she had simply wanted to stop thinking altogether.

Now the grade is steep and Margaret moves in short bursts downhill, catching herself on the trunk of one huge tree and then pushing off to the next. The forest here has never been logged. Slow growth and the passage of animals and weather, seasons, that is change here. As she grabs at a spruce, a whiskey jack screeches from the top boughs and glides to the next tree. Margaret sees the bird caught in a sunbeam, perfectly silhouetted, and with a down of fire lining each feather.

Margaret's bare legs burn with scratches. She smiles. She is beginning to feel hunger as well as thirst. She touches the pocket that holds the chocolate bar, and gently rests her warm hand on her stomach. She is certain that she is more than halfway to the lake. The late evening sun is sliding across the valley. Margaret knows that the brief night will be cold. But she is imagining how she will make herself a shelter from spruce boughs, how there will be grass by the lake, and how she will make a bed and cover herself with dry grass until morning.

Montana Mountain

Patricia Robertson

1

Imagining ourselves trees,
                    or birds
we are called to stone.

2

Stone threads our spines together.

3

In the stone houses
the miners made,
the doorways lead nowhere,
bound by boulders.

4

Stepping through
from one air into another
you vanish
turn
a pickaxe over your shoulder.

Blockade

Erling Friis-Baastad

I never intended to live
so far from the sea.
The boy I was
could not have fathomed

life on a mere river,
could not have fathomed
mere life. It is as if
the tide has gone out

and out from it
leaving dry flats
and fears and duties
while overhead

the same stars pass
again and again —
a flotilla that flies
the enemy's standard.

Towards Evening

Erling Friis-Baastad

As words fall, I learn

        Shameless I arrive

to rename the warm objects

        at your words, gasping

in your welcoming hut

        through your mouth

One is wrist

        You are that first wave

which turns

and that last

to reveal a cupped palm

to break over my face

from which my wavering double

My hand clutches up

pours himself

into your book

while attempting to navigate

through wine and wood

and stone

Wood Spoken

Erling Friis-Baastad

We are learning to bend close
and reach down to these;
logs, sticks, even boards

(though others have had their way
with them) recall home
and greener days.

We are being called upon
to condense, to dip twigs
in primary colours,

trace one bright line
across each life,
or carve two letters
into the weathered wall
of some abandoned hut.

our initials will serve.
there are already too many words,
too many names for that
which refuses to grow on trees.

The Twenty-first Century Log Cabin

Dianne Homan

When I was five, I made my first attempt to pee outside. I went behind some concealing bushes, bared my posterior, squatted, and peed right into my shorts. After years of playing in the woods and going on camping and hiking trips, I became more adept at this skill. Then I moved to a log cabin in the Yukon. "You can pee in the slop bucket," my husband said. But after a lifetime of shutting a washroom door or going behind a concealing bush, peeing in the slop bucket was a bit too much public exposure for me. I slipped on my Sorels and a jacket, went outside to a private spot, and peed right on my untied bootlaces.

Since then, my boundaries between public and private have shifted. Peeing in the slop bucket is no longer a problem. Living in a small log cabin requires

facing and paying attention to the earthy details of life
that in a civilized house can simply be flushed away.

When I first moved into what had been my husband's bachelor home, he and I lived in one room with
the wood cookstove and kitchen counter in one corner,
the table and bookshelf in another corner, and the
narrow bed in a third. It's a good thing this was the
honeymoon phase of our relationship. My husband
borrowed a horse and dragged in logs from dead trees
that winter, and the following spring, in a one-month
building frenzy, added two rooms to our cabin. It felt like
a mansion. We now had a low-ceilinged upstairs bedroom and a second room on the main floor that served
as a living room, office, and library. This side room was
dubbed "the feminist room" in response to my amused
first reaction upon visiting my husband-to-be in his
wilderness cabin. "It's such a guy place!" I laughed as I
noticed the bow and arrows hanging from one ceiling
beam, the fishing rod on another, and the furniture and
floorboards crafted with a chain saw and covered with
animal hides.

Since our first months of married life, we've had
ongoing discussions about additions and improvements
to the cabin that will help to ensure continued marital
compatibility. We have found that there are many
choices to be made as we adjust to the demands of
different jobs, the realities of getting older, and the
temptations of newly available small-scale and earth-
friendly technologies.

As we researched our options at the public library, we found books about log-building, about vacation homes, about seaside cottages, and about wilderness cabins, all of which led to a discussion about our choice of nomenclature for our little nest. One author, B. Allan Mackie, a renowned expert in log-building, chooses not to call his structures "log cabins." To him, there is an implication of slavery (as in *Uncle Tom's Cabin*) and of confinement (as in this quote from *Macbeth*: "But now I am cabin'd, cribbed, confin'd, bound to saucy doubts and fears.") Mackie seems to think that, as civilized beings, we should have matured beyond our fascination with the rustic. He is impressed by enormous and glamorous log buildings like Montebello, the CPR hotel built in Quebec in 1930 from ten thousand giant cedar logs. It would cost as much to stay in that hotel for a few nights as it cost to build our home.

Some builders of back-to-nature dwellings prefer the term "cottage." Usually, cottages are quaint little getaway places for stressed suburbanites. A few of our neighbours around the lake have built what might aptly be termed cottages. But these small frame structures are nothing like the weekend cottage the hugely wealthy Vanderbilt family erected at Newport, Rhode Island, in the early twentieth century. It was five storeys tall, had seventy rooms, and was furnished with imported tapestries, alabaster pillars, marble bathtubs, and ornate fireplaces, on one of which was inscribed the motto,

"Little do I care for wealth." My husband and I could carve that motto into one of the logs over our homemade barrel heating stove. But it wouldn't have nearly the same effect.

Our cabin could be called a log house, but B. Allan Mackie said the first log house he built was "only 700 square feet." Ours is 635 square feet and doesn't have an indoor toilet, although we discuss the possibility of putting in a composting toilet for our senior years if our wrinkled posteriors become too sensitive to a cold outhouse seat. No, our home probably doesn't qualify as a house, so, to avoid confusion, we'll just call it a cabin.

But there are other more meaningful and compli- cated choices to be made about log cabin life. When we arrive home on any given evening, we don't reach inside the door and flick an electric light switch. We don't check phone messages or turn up a thermostat. We don't run water out of a tap or open a refrigerator door, although we do store perishable groceries in a plywood coolbox that we access by lifting two sections of the heavy chainsawed floorboards. We have chosen to do without some things and have found interesting alterna- tives to others.

My relationship with modern conveniences has changed over the years. In the early seventies, when I was living in West Virginia, I discovered the delights of getting water from its natural source. A friend of mine owned an old, unoccupied farmhouse five miles from the nearest town, and I would bike there and stay a few days. A little stone spring house sat just beyond the back door of the weathered grey main building. It was always cool and dim inside, even when the summer heat outside rose in waves through the humid air. Clear water flowed steadily out of a narrow pipe and fell into a shallow pool, the sound of it like a repeated mantra. I poured the water over my skin and drank cups of it until I felt almost as transparent as the water itself.

Water feels the same in the Yukon. My body appreciates the cleansing power of water without chemicals, and my mind appreciates the slower, more flowing pace determined by physical distance, muscular effort, and weather.

At our cabin, it takes at least three minutes to get water. We have two five-gallon plastic buckets that we carry down the trail to the creek where it flows out of the lake. In summer, it's just a matter of dipping and hauling, for which long arms and a strong back are helpful. In winter, there's the added challenge of chopping the water hole open every day with an axe. Our neighbours bring their water containers to our winter water hole on toboggans, because they've discovered that pump systems freeze up and auger tips get dull quickly.

"Simplicity is the key to success" was stressed in one of the books we read about cabins and cottages. We could carve that motto into the log above our water bucket shelf. In a log cabin lifestyle, nothing could be simpler than dipping fresh water for drinking, cooking, cleaning, and bathing, and then dumping the used water outside, where the fireweed seem to delight in the extra nutrients. When we go away in the winter, we just empty our buckets and kettles of water, let the stove go out, and leave. No frozen pipes, no cracked containers, no clogged drains.

Sometimes, though, our need for a higher level of technology becomes apparent. When forest fires threatened the cabins around Fox Lake three summers ago, we looked into a pump system, because we knew that the old stories of bucket brigades usually didn't have happy endings. For a few thousand dollars, we bought a small gasoline-powered pump, three enormous sections of fire hose, and three sprinkler heads that sit atop our roof, the roof of my brother-in-law's cabin next door, and the workshop roof. In case of a forest fire around our mountain lake, we can soak our entire property, then load the pump and a hose into a canoe and paddle over to spray the neighbours' cabins and cottages.

We discovered another time-saving benefit of this system as we tested it one summer day. My husband and I used to spend more than half an hour every other evening giving the garden a good drink with watering cans — a task for which we felt the pace of muscular effort was too slow, especially when the mosquitoes were biting. Now we simply start the pump, aim the hose nozzle at the sky over the vegetable patch or the potato patch, take a firm stance, and open the valve.

Three minutes later, the garden is drenched, and everything in the immediate area, including us, is dripping,
that lovely mantra-like sound sweetening the evening
air.

The old farmhouse in West Virginia, which seems to
have been a training ground for my current life, didn't
have electricity. Making do without power was an adventure; it was romantic. But when I moved to Portland,
Oregon, in 1979, I became aware of humanity's less-
than-perfect relationship with electricity and added
some rationality to my hitherto emotional response to
the question of plugging in. Seventy miles east of
Portland, the wide Columbia River is blocked by The
Dalles Dam, an impressive concrete structure with a
viewing room from which one can watch salmon climb
the fish ladder. Then, one day in the gallery of the
Oregon Historical Society, I saw mesmerizing old brown-
tinted photos of Celilo Indians fishing from rickety
wooden platforms over a raging wild waterfall — a
waterfall with salmon jumping up it, a waterfall that
was swallowed into silence and flat water by the big
hydroelectric dam.

Thirty miles downstream on the Columbia River
west of Portland is the Trojan nuclear power plant,
which in the seventies and eighties was the main
provider of electricity to the city. When I first arrived in
Portland, the plant was closed down for much-needed
repairs, a situation I found less than comforting considering the highly toxic materials involved. As a protest

against nuclear power, I formed a righteous plan to call the power company and tell them to switch off my electricity as soon as Trojan resumed operations. I watched The Oregonian for mention of this event, sure that something that figured so significantly in my worldview would be headline news. Months later, telling a friend of my resolve, I was told that Trojan had re-started weeks before, and yes, there had been a few lines mentioning the fact in the back of the Metro section of the paper. The critical moment had passed, and so did my earnest resolution. It was simply easier to continue using that which flowed into my house so invisibly and imperceptibly.

When I moved to the log cabin in the Yukon, it was outfitted with propane lamps. Arriving home after dark meant dropping packs and bundles, fumbling for matches on the windowsill, and striking one while reaching with the other hand for the knob that would start the flow of propane into the lamp. The golden light was adequate for most tasks, and the glass and brass fixtures were lovely, mounted on the curved faces of logs. But as my husband and I reached middle age, we started to feel some eye strain, which we knew would be lessened by brighter light. We invested a few thou-sand dollars more in a solar panel, which is attached to the top of a tall log tripod behind the cabin. The cable runs under the bottom log of the back wall, up the corner of the feminist room, to a little platform at the top of the bedroom steps. There sit two large twelve-volt batteries, a voltmeter, a fuse box, an invertor, a battery charge regulator, and other unnamed boxes, wires, and switches. There's nothing invisible or imperceptible about this electric power system. I've learned to watch the voltmeter on short winter days, and if the needle swings down to twelve I turn off the electric lamp, or the CD player, or the sewing machine, or the typewriter, my current inventory of electrical gadgets. When I consider buying a new gadget, I read the small print on the back to make sure it doesn't draw more than one amp. That's not much.

My husband and his brother talk about hooking up a micro-hydro system on the creek that runs by our property. They fantasize about a wind generator up on the ridge, within sight of the big windmills on Haeckel Hill. They've heard about a new way of generating electricity from the heat that flows through the stovepipe. We probably will have more power someday. It would be nice to be able to plug in our cars on cold winter days rather than using the propane tiger torch or a pan of glowing charcoal briquets. It would be nice to iron summer clothes better than my butane iron can manage or to use a food processor instead of a grater and an egg beater. And the guys would appreciate using power tools in the workshop. But when the day comes that these modern conveniences become realistic possibilities for us, we might just sit back and rethink whether we don't really prefer life the way we've been living it, without all those extras.

One appliance I will never be tempted to buy is a replacement for my wood cookstove. At first it made me very nervous. I had visions of blackened masses being pulled from the oven and of being drenched with sweat every time I cooked a meal. The first fear disappeared quickly as I learned how forgiving wood cookstoves are. The temperature doesn't have to be exact, and the cooking time is even more flexible. Breads and cakes come out moist and golden, although I do have to rotate them a few times to guarantee that they're even in colour and texture. As for the sweat, opening doors and windows, or removing my long-johns seems to do the trick.

One item of technology that comes up regularly in our home improvement discussions is the telephone, especially now that my husband has started a small business that requires frequent phone contact with clients. We haven't been impressed with the options we've seen so far. Two former neighbours who had cell phones were often seen driving around the neighbour-hood in their trucks, trying to find a spot from which they could make a call. Often, my brother-in-law's phone doesn't work or gets such a crackly signal that a con-versation is nearly impossible anyway. Radio phones are a noisy intrusion if one values a quiet life as we do. Soon enough, satellite phones will be simple and inexpensive and will have the Internet possibilities that telephones on the phone line have now. My husband and I have decided we can wait until then.

If we lived in town, I think decisions like these would be made quickly and spontaneously. But in our log cabin, we take time to weigh, to measure, to mull, to value. We talked about a fire protection system for years before we bought it. Same with the solar panel. Speed and convenience are not all that inviting to us. Quiet, beauty, and walking softly on the earth are.

Architect Frank Lloyd Wright encouraged home builders to move "as far out as you can get" and to create "organic" dwellings. When you stand across Jackson Lake from our place, you barely notice the cabin; its log walls and sod roof nestle comfortably into the curve of the hill. The white moose antlers crowning the high cache and the solar panel on top of its log tripod will catch your eye, though. They illustrate the kinds of choices we've made in the pioneer spirit of the twenty-first century.

Michael Reynolds has lived in Whitehorse since leaving Ontario in 1995, and has crossed that distance by Greyhound on more than one occasion. This is his first published story, though he has published poetry in *Out of Service, Ice Floe* and *The Fiddlehead*. Presently he is working on a series of long poems.

Patricia Robertson's short story collection, *City of Orphans*, was shortlisted for the British Columbia Book Prizes, and her poem "Inukshuk" was a runner-up in the George Woodcock Poetry Competition. She is co-editor of *Writing North: An Anthology of Contemporary Yukon Writers* and teaches creative writing in Whitehorse.

Born in Norway in 1950, **Erling Friis-Baastad** has spent much of his adult life in the Yukon. His poems have appeared internationally in many magazines and in several anthologies and chapbooks. His most recent work, *The Exile House*, was published by salmonpoetry in Ireland.

Dianne Homan, for the past twenty-some years, has been a dancer, a coyote-ish thing to be north of sixty. Now she's turning her creative energies to writing. She is the author of a children's book, *In Christina's Toolbox*.

Lead Dog Dreams

Paul Davis

She wakes with the dawn,
puts logs in the stove,
shrugs on a two-dollar Cowichan sweater
from the Sally Ann,
and gives her dog team the first hug of the day.

There's six of them out there,
seven if you count the one on loan,
but only one who is allowed to sleep in the cabin.

We sleep together, head to toe, and nose to tail,
the three of us,
She Who Feeds Us,
The Lead Dog,
and The Visiting Artist.

None of us smell,
which is kind of remarkable,
as we curl up in our down bags,
and fur coats,
groping about,
fur, holding hands, snouts, feet.
A comfortable tangle,
where the inter-species boundaries
slip a little bit...

Orion beckons in the night sky,
as I write my name in the snow
with pee,
but give up after the first letter.

I sneak back into bed,
feeling my way in the dark,
fingers probing for paws, wayward dog tails,
potential lovers' hair, misplaced feet,
furry snouts and flashlights.

The Lead Dog rolls over,
and lays her snout on my arm.
My arm is tickled by her moving eyes
as she chases endless hares.

Salt & Pepper Greybeard

Murray Munn

The Bohemians are back
    with each generation
    beard-proud, perfect
Che & Cat glaring at new poems in every
coffeeshop corner,
horn-rimmed grrls on each arm.

Static line parachuting and crossing roadblocks in Africa form part of **Paul Davis**'s life experiences. His day jobs have been as varied, his current racket being part-time teaching when he's not full-time writing in Whitehorse.

Murray Munn grew up in Saskatchewan and received an honours degree in English in 1985 from McGill University. He has written adult fiction, plays, children's literature, poetry and nonfiction. Murray is currently at work on a new play, and has two children's stories in the works.

Variations on Gestalt:
A Monologue in E

Lawrie Crawford

Variations on Gestalt *has been performed at the Brave New Playwrights Festival in Vancouver and Brave New Works in Whitehorse. The musical score was composed by Owen Boomfield and has been produced in two variations, one with four actors and cello, and the other with three actors and tuba.*

I am twisted/tormented with the pull-push of desire; contorted by loves long past. Safety has fallen away.

I swallow at air, and gasp.

I might never hear from you again.

The impending: "You don't have any new e-mail,"
for days and days upon a time (though less than a
day has passed). I know it was stupid to push the
send button as I re-read my nonsense from yesterday. How could I have said that?

What was I thinking of?   *"DO YOU ASTRO-TRAVEL?"*
Am I crazy?

Then again — it had purpose.

I wanted to know if that full-size, full-bodied fig-
ment under the covers beside me last Sunday
night was your manifestation, rather (of course)
than me, just ... making you up.

Just making you up from a kiss ...

After all, kisses can make you crazy, you know.

Perfectly scaled delusions of a man in my bed,
true to the touch, and a fast-forwarded memory.

It was only a kiss.

Men fantasize. Women hallucinate.

But I really want you to know that I touched you,
and felt you present *with* me.

So astro-travel was all I could think of! Like, what am I supposed to say? "Did you know you were in my bed last night?"

After all, we'd barely just met. One kiss. (I'd recovered my breath, steadied my quivering body against a dust-caked car as the music rocked on in the Pipeline Club; the sky still light at four o'clock in the morning.)

One kiss in Valdez, Alaska. I speeded back to Whitehorse; you scrounged a ride to Anchorage.

Maybe I imagined you with me.

But the odd thing was — it wasn't when I wanted you that you showed up. I hadn't expected you.

That's the strange part. You startled me. Then, I was   overcome.

That used to happen with a man I knew.

A man I knew! Who am I kidding? The love of my life, who pulled me inside out and left me an empty shell.

I could feel his hands when we were thousands of miles apart. But never did I see him like I saw and felt you last night. This was new. Your body was in my bed.

That is why this   is   so   scary.

So, do you astro-travel? I suppose it's a natural question, considering …

Considering … we just talked.

Considering … I was naked under my long silk dress when you bent your head down to kiss me gently with your full   soft   lips.

Why do I note them?

I assess men by their lips, you know.

"Never trust a man with thin lips." Is the inverse true?   Perhaps.

Your lips opened me into trusting you.

Something that I know I never should do, especially when I know nothing.

Nothing. I trusted the opening you offered. But I know nothing. Who do you live with? Who do you care for? I never asked.

Maybe I overreacted.

I should never click on "send."

I can hear you now.

"Bad. Bad girl. Go away and I won't write you any more."

I'm so much more fun in person, gently joking away the fears and anxiety.

That light, early nervousness of possibility.

"Susceptibility can be a sweet thing," you said.

But you don't know the half of it!

I'm at risk in text. Forced to an honesty that is a naked hell.

I come across that way in print — without the chuckles and the winks and the hand on your thigh, or ankle against your calf under the table, to reassure you that you're safe with me.

You are really, very safe with me.   If

                              you are really *with* me.

* * *

I need a response. (Even a reaction would do.)

I wait and hold my breath this time.

Then I gasp —

I think that perhaps, just maybe … that you are not quite so safe with me.

I live without a railing, you know.

That's why I don't invite many people over.

They're shocked at the narrow ledge left hanging from that day of demolition. A thin strip of old living room floor, 39 inches wide and 15 feet straight down, overlooking an inspired renovation, unrealized.

It doesn't bother me though. I just hang on, and lean out …

Let it all hang out! I used to be really casual. Once, a single doctor was chatting me up at a potluck, seeming really interested and all that. I told him I eat graham wafer and butter sand-wiches for dinner, and he took off before I fin-ished the next sentence.

I think you're a guy who eats cold pizza for breakfast.

See, I'm more cautious now. I think living with this narrow ledge has helped.

It used to be splintered and ragged from the teeth of my husband's chainsaw as he fed the rest of the house to a D9 cat, December 2, 1992.

I smoothed the ripped edge with time.

Down below is where the walls fell on me.

I was trying to tear them apart and it happened incredibly fast. Forty-five feet long of spaced 2 x 6 studs, 15 feet high, sheathed with plywood, crashed towards me.

The sound was so loud! Everything flattened around me, and I found myself safe in a hole in the wall — in the space planned for a doorway.

I was fine ...   but, I couldn't find my dog.

Those are the times I go a little crazy.

When I don't know something, like where my kids are in the middle of the night, or why you haven't written. Damn! I'd get like that before he'd come home with his shirt buttoned-up wrong.

I couldn't lift the walls. I was afraid my dog was underneath. Was he hurt but alive?

Hurt but alive.

I've left men like that before. They say it's my
fault. I used to believe them, but now I think I
just ...   well, I found them that way.

My dog was hiding by the lake. He's more like me,
and only barks when people leave.

I remember you saying, "The success of a relationship isn't in its duration." Very 60s and all
that, but my dog will look like he's attacking when
you try to leave ... that is ... if you ever come over.

But I don't want to make you nervous.

I *had* to take down the walls — there was no
rebar in the concrete footings my husband and
I had laid for the new addition. Oh, I know he
knew better, but he was drinking by then — he
didn't care. I cared, but he was the journeyman
carpenter. We poured the concrete in a day, but
the walls went up more slowly.

Later, all these old guys shook their heads when
they looked at the cracks in the footings. They
said, "You can't build a structure that lasts, not
without a good foundation."

It wasn't anything that could be fixed;

once the lies were laid down.

I got rid of most of the dangerous stuff.

I suppose crowbars, nail pullers, and rubber mallets are a sort of mid-range therapy: between splitting wood, when you visualize your lover's face in the concentric rings and aim for the core; and pounding pillows with plastic bats, coddled by strangers who share your pain.

Those are usually the same strangers who yearn to become astro-travellers and sign up for workshops on their vacations. I don't want you to think I'm like them.

It was an incredible amount of work ...

I pulled and pried nails from the rafters and joists and walls of the framed-in shell. It took all the strength I had — forcing out those obsessive metal shards that bound him and me so tightly.

I burned the wood when the nails wouldn't come out. Some of the lumber I stacked, some I sold; scavengers and thieves took the rest. I grew tanned and strong doing it, and rested for a long time after.

I grew to feeling comfortable with the walls gone.

Safe.

Now I'm exposed!

> Your kiss tripped a main nerve somewhere. Created an opening I'm falling into. Openings long to be filled. And I don't want to long for anything.

> Part of me wants nothing of this.   The rest of me knows no railing …

> A kiss to the abyss …

> In free fall.

Who cares?

> I've learned, upon impact, that lies hurt more than any hard truth ever can.

> So … I don't know if you're safe with me. Or if I'll ever hear from you again.

It's a scary thing.

> Is need a burden already?

*   *   *

> Willows are growing through the gravel now. Fireweed camouflages scars from the tracks of the D9 that tore the house apart. A pile of charred and rusty nails lies in a mound of ashes.

Only the cracked ruin of the unstable foundation
rings the space where the addition was to be.

Was to be.

No addition now — just a small space with a
narrow ledge.

An edge with a great view.

That's all it ever is,

this love stuff.

Lawrie Crawford, who has lived in the Yukon for twenty-five years, writes plays, essays, and sports journalism. She studied in the creative non-fiction program at UBC.

Karen Schneider has wandered the world looking for somewhere to call home, and has found it in the most surprising of places. She has learned to keep her shoes on when she goes out dancing.

Michele Genest was born and raised in Toronto and moved to Whitehorse in 1994. A playwright and journalist, she is also the co-author, with Erling Friis-Bastaad, of *Whitehorse: The First 200 Million Years*.

Dean Eyre was born in Saskatoon and moved to Whitehorse in 1992. He is the co-editor and publisher of *Out Of Service* magazine.

Yvette Nolan's plays include *BLADE, Job's Wife, Video, Annie Mae's Movement*, and *Donne In. Shakedown Shakespeare*, her co-creation with Philip Adams, toured Yukon communities in spring of 1997. She is the president of the Playwrights Union of Canada. Most of her currently resides in Nova Scotia; her heart remains in the north.

Frozen Buttocks
and Frontier Fantasies

Karen Schneider

We arrived in Whitehorse in early May 1996 with no intention of staying longer than a summer. Planning to reach the Yukon before all the summer tourists, Melissa, Ruth, and I had left the Fraser Valley three days earlier, dressed in shorts and T-shirts and sassy early summer tans, only to find snow still on the ground. Now, we were wearing all our clothes to bed to ward off the chill long enough to fall asleep. Mornings became a routine of bribery and blackmail to see who would be the first out of the tent to start a fire for coffee. Then, like a herd of horses, we would stand around snorting and stomping to bring our frozen feet back to life. We paced the town with red noses and cast-off gloves from the Salvation Army, handing out hastily written résumés outlining our dubious work histories.

Before leaving for Whitehorse, we had waited for Melissa, the only one of us with any real responsibilities, to finish her semester at university. Ruth was staying with her family in Toronto after having spent six months in Brazil searching for voodoo, finding instead street urchins, sambas, and love in the barrios. I'd passed the winter on one of the Gulf Islands, watching the rain that had driven Ruth to warmer climes. Holed up in my cliff-top cabin, I got to know my cat and all the colours of the ocean. We were all ready for a change, all ripe for adventure. On a whim, I called Melissa and asked if she wanted to go to the Yukon for the summer. Then I called Ruth with our newly hatched plans.

Three weeks later, the three of us stood on the side of the highway, dancing to the beat of Melissa's boom box, or the less reliable rhythms produced on my African djembe. It took us three days and four rides to get to Whitehorse. On the outskirts of Watson Lake, a young couple, also hitchhiking, approached us from their pitch farther up the highway. They had been there for three days; no one had even slowed down. We sighed and fell to bargaining over who should go buy groceries for our long encampment on the highway. We never had time to decide: a camper pulled up, and we were on our way to Whitehorse. We hadn't even raised a thumb.

In Whitehorse, we were dropped off at Food Fair, which caused us a moment of alarm. There had been no room for strip malls in our visions of this northern world. We quickly escaped what struck us as the ugliness of a typical mid-sized Canadian town and found our way to the Yukon River. The river winds past the territorial government buildings and along the eastern edge of the downtown core. At the northern end of town, it seems to slow down, to ramble past a row of squatters' shacks that, in all their dilapidated glory, gave Whitehorse the real-people-must-live-here, frontier feeling that we were hoping for. This ramshackle neighbourhood made me think of John Steinbeck's *Tortilla Flat* — we later learned that locals called this area Whiskey Flats, which only strengthened my first impression. And we, like the characters in that book, could always rustle up the coin for a bottle of red wine.

Often we ended up huddling in the Talisman Café on Second Avenue to look over the meagre column of classified ads in the local newspaper. We were rarely in competition for jobs. Melissa had experience ranging from cooking in a country bar to caring for autistic children; I had worked landscaping the last few summers and was looking for something that would take me outdoors; and Ruth, well, Ruth would try her hand at anything. We were optimistic about landing the high-paying jobs we had been told were so easy to come by up here. That they failed to materialize right away just meant that we should take a little holiday.

One sky-blue day, when the sun at last felt warm on our faces, we set out from town, walking with nothing but jackets, a camera, and a few bananas to snack on. After spending too many nights getting acquainted with the bar scene in Whitehorse, Ruth had declared that we were all in need of some healthy activity. We headed out toward Miles Canyon, to see where the paths took us. We talked, laughed, and sang our way there and back, through the miniature forest that seemed like a fairy world after the West Coast rainforest we were accustomed to. We were delighted with the fact that just five minutes out of town, we felt like we were in the heart of a vast wilderness — no roads, no people, the possibility of bears lurking behind every bush.

Later we went down to the river, back to the ramshackle homes that seemed to preserve another era of Whitehorse history. Looking for a friend of a friend, we fell into conversation with a few fellows sharing a bottle of wine on the riverbank. They knew him, they said, but he wasn't around anymore. Not wanting us to leave disappointed, one of them offered me a ride on his motorcycle. Eyeing the half-full bottle of wine and calculating its possible effects, I jumped on and we tore down the riverside path, then out onto the streets. We flew up First Avenue with huge grins on our faces, until the driver saw a police car. He quickly turned around and headed back to the river.

Whitehorse's isolation brought out a bit of the wild in us all. The fresh air and the limitless horizon infected our spirits, and we whooped it up at night with proper frontier town enthusiasm. We danced daring sambas in bare feet, until the bar owners objected — not to our dancing, but to our feet — although I'm sure our girl-on-girl moves raised a few eyebrows. We delighted in stumbling wearily along the river in the light of the midnight sun, under a glorious pink sky that washed away the smoky grime of our intoxication.

Early-morning tumbles out of the tent and into the Yukon River became my routine. My hazy vision sans contact lenses kept me ignorant of the proximity of a well-travelled path on the opposite bank of the river that afforded anyone walking down that path a clear view of my morning ablutions. I might not have cared. A season among hippies and former draft dodgers on my Gulf Island had done much to cure me of bodily inhibition.

One gin-and-tonic evening we fell in with a group of young men on the same adventure-seeking wavelength, who, it turned out, were building a raft to recreate a gold-fevered journey down the Yukon River to the Bering Sea. They were doing it fully sponsored, with money from the National Geographic Society and the CBC, and with barrels of food from a variety of sources. Talk of food led to a challenge: who could cook up the best meal over a campfire? It was decided that the six boys would give it their best shot the next night, and they invited us to their raft to share the meal. We, of course, would bring the wine.

Arriving at the bank of the river, we admired the craftsmanship of their raft, which boasted a full-size wall tent with ample room for a deck party remaining.

Anchored to the side of the raft, cooling in the still-icy
Yukon River, were at least two dozen beers and a large
bottle of white wine. We set into them with a gusto
inspired by the freshness of both the night air and the
boys we were dining with.

Dinner was a vegetarian curry of the finest order,
accompanied by a bottled mango chutney which, given
the hard-and-fast rules of our campfire cook-off —
everything made by hand, over fire — should have been
considered cheating, but wasn't. You simply can't make
mango chutney in a frying pan, in early May, on a raft
on the Yukon River. We produced a dessert of baked
bananas, sizzled in a cast-iron pan, all syrupy in ginger
and sugar and honey, served with ice cream kept cool
in the last remnants of snow on the shore. The wine
and beer were perfect accompaniments to the meal,
judging by their speedy disappearance as we ate.
Guitars, drums, and cameras came out; so did a
surprise bottle of Glenlivet.

The rest of the evening was a haze of glowing fire
and freezing buttocks, as we all speed-stripped in the
biting night air and dove into the frigid river. What
happened after that bracing dip is a blur of silliness,
cigars, and an impromptu wrestling match. At the start
of our journey, Melissa, Ruth, and I had established a
tradition of wrestling at bedtime for the warmest spot in
the tent, the middle. Despite the ample bed space and
the warmth of the wall tent, we saw no reason to forego
tradition.

The next morning, in the slow drawl of a hangover, Pete, the most innocent and charming of the boys, was heard to say of Melissa, "Wow, man. She's the coolest girl I ever met! It took her seven seconds to take her clothes off, and seven hours to get them all back on!" We never saw the pictures from the rolls of film they shot that night; either they were not very good photographers under the influence of single-malt scotch, or they didn't want to embarrass us with our overexposure.

We fell in love with our new northern home over that summer of 1996. Whitehorse felt welcoming, safe, and full of possibilities. We were enchanted by this jewel of small-town Canada, isolated and protected by thousands of kilometres of boreal forest. Life was lived freestyle here; you never knew what might happen.

Our escapades continued unabated for several weeks before we began to get the first inkling of how small a town Whitehorse really is. It dawned on us that the people who were witnessing our evening revelries were the same people to whom we were applying for jobs. For Melissa and me, this was an immediate signal to tone things down, or at least to cover them up. Ruth had a different take on the matter: well, if they've seen me in the bar and they're still giving me an interview, things can't be that bad. She did end up with the most interesting job, electromagnetic surveying for a mining company out in the bush near Finlayson Lake, where there was no reputation to uphold.

Of the three of us, I stayed on in Whitehorse. In time, the faces on dance floors and at interviews grew familiar — some of them became friends, whose lives and stories give the town more character and depth than I was capable of perceiving during my first summer in the north.

Whitehorse has become my home. After a decade of travelling, I have surprised myself by settling into life in the north. I have grown roots here, in the permafrost soil. Roots that not only withstand the long, cold winters but are born of them. Born of friendships that are nurtured in front of cosy fires and inspired under the night sky, where magic lights dance, it seems, for our spirits.

A Wilderness in the City

Michele Genest

I grew up in Toronto, a city scored with deep ravines. Creeks run through the ravines, and there are
rivers, too, like the Don in the east and the Humber in
the west. When I was small, my parents used to take
my brothers and sister and me to one of those ravines
for picnics on weekend afternoons. The ravine had a
name — it was in fact a park — but to us it was always
"The End of Broadway." Broadway was the name of the
big street our little cul-de-sac led to, and Broadway
ended at the gates of the park, at the gates of our
entrance into another world, a place removed from the
city, dark and hidden and lush.

Prosaic-sounding now, "The End of Broadway" when
I was little conjured all the romance and possibility of
Shangri-La. There was a wild melancholy in the name. It

contained our deep response to the wide, shallow stream that ran under bridges and through poplars and maples at the heart of the ravine. We played there endlessly, digging into the clay banks, making dams with stones, and looking for fish in the clear brown water. The melancholy came from our wish for real wilderness, our knowledge that the park we played in wasn't the real thing. We longed for the real thing.

That longing had another source, I think, which comes with living in a town or a city: the feeling of exile from Nature, of being ousted from the Garden. Urban theorists from Jane Jacobs to Tony Hiss have written about the sense of alienation that comes when city dwellers are deprived of grass and trees. Hiss carries it one step further: not only do urbanites need parks, they need farmland mixed with woods and meadows, and they need wilderness; it's fundamental to their well-being to have access to the wild.

My brothers and sister and I had grass and trees, but our stream stank, like every stream and river in Toronto. We played in it anyway, because we had to. It was the closest we could come to wilderness.

Now I live in Whitehorse, surrounded by wilderness on all sides. You can stand anywhere in the city, look up and see mountains of incredible beauty. You can drive out of town for twenty minutes in any direction, hike a couple of kilometres, and find yourself in the middle of a wilderness so real it's scary. You could die in that wilderness, if you made just a few small mistakes — if you got lost without food or matches, or you had a bad encounter with a bear. It's partly the possibility of death that makes the wilderness wild.

When I first arrived in Whitehorse, I lived in a cabin on the Mayo road. A five-minute walk from my door and I was deep in the woods. Every spring, bears wandered into the small compound of twenty or so cabins; we had coyotes and foxes and grouse, too. We also had rabbits — domestic rabbits, a pet project of the woman who owned the property. She held to the bizarre principle that where rabbits flourished, moose and caribou would follow. Mostly the rabbits got eaten by the cats and dogs that she prohibited, but that tenants sneaked in.

The two years I spent in that small enclave of cabins and rabbits and the occasional bear were idyllic. But necessity prompted a move into town, and there was the rub. Whitehorse, like most northern towns, is hideously ugly. Sprawling, unplanned, and dotted with buildings slapped together with no regard for beauty, Whitehorse is a misshapen carbuncle in a gorgeous setting. The town is an affront to the beauty that surrounds it, and bad town planning has ensured that whatever fragments of natural beauty that have managed to withstand the encroachment of urban blight are being paved over or filled in, one by one. Except for the clay cliffs.

At one time, the clay cliffs were the banks of the Yukon River; now they contain the river and the city, they define the edges of the valley we live in. I live at their base, on an unpaved road at the west end of town, in the oldest residential part of the city. The houses look like cottages. From the room I'm sitting in I can look up over my right shoulder and see a line of white against the sky, the knife edge of a snowy cornice, the tips of spruce trees with nothing but blue behind them. I can walk into the living room and look at Grey Mountain, and very lovely it is, but the clay cliffs are right here behind me. In five minutes I can be on top of them, with ravens wheeling around my head and the wind blowing and the city far below and actually looking almost picturesque, if it's nighttime and Christmas and the coloured lights are up.

The cliffs are a little bit of wilderness in the city; they satisfy the longing to be elsewhere and the need for something wild. Coyotes, foxes, and sometimes people sleep in the woods there. The trees provide a haven for the secret lives of animals and people — the animals make tracks, the people leave cigarette butts and broken glass and condoms.

Like the real wilderness, the clay cliffs are not safe, or tame. Hidden by the trees in the gullies, people commit secret and sometimes terrible acts. A woman was murdered there last spring, by someone she knew. Her belongings were strewn across the snow and the mud. A man and his dog found them. Since then, people walking alone stare uneasily into the trees, look over their shoulders, feel the backs of their necks.

There is good reason to be watchful, just as there is in the bush.

A dog is good company up there, and people who have dogs are especially fond of the cliffs. You can let them run free, far from the gimlet eye of the city dog-catcher who roams the streets in an unmarked van, on the make for the cash each unleashed dog brings in. To get up to the cliffs, with or without dogs, you climb through Puckett's Gulch at the top of Black and Alexander Streets. Or you can take one of the many tracks that climb through the woods, tracks made by kids with snowboards in the winter, heading up to jump cornices, or by kids hiding bottles under their jackets in the summer, looking for a private place to let out the wildness in their blood.

Whichever way you take, it's a steep climb — the transition from city to cliffs requires exertion. In some places you have to hang on to branches and pull yourself up. Coming down, you hang on to branches so as not to fall and slide fast downhill, on clay or ice or thick, viscous mud, depending on the season.

It's hard to describe the feeling of release, the lifting of the spirit that accompanies your arrival at the top. Like the gates at The End of Broadway, the climb leads to somewhere else, where the ache for wilderness is both awakened and (almost, but never fully) satisfied. In winter, the wind whistles down across the plateau, shaping the snow into sharp-edged drifts or hard-packed pillows that curl over the cliff edge. The wind is constant, summer or winter, whipping fine sand or snow into your eyes, and stirring up the scent of river and woods. In fall and spring, the transition seasons, you can freeze and bake on the same walk. In spring, the smell of cottonwood and poplar buds is intoxicating — both balsamic and floral, it floods the body with nostalgia for a place you've never been.

The deep satisfaction of walking along the cliffs, looking down on the city or north and south along the river valley, has something to do with being able to see, unimpeded. There's nothing in the way on the clifftops. You're far enough from the mountains that they become a place where the eyes rest before turning to sweep back down along the valley. At its bottom there is the river, never quite frozen over in winter, gleaming cold green on grey days or glittering blue and electric in the sun, signifying movement, possibility, and change.

More than a hundred years ago, the river brought the man who built the first road up to the cliffs from the brand-new town of Whitehorse. Puckett's Gulch is named after William Puckett, one of Whitehorse's first merchants. He had a house on Wood Street, two blocks from the gulch. But Puckett didn't build the road up the gulch that was named after him. Antoine Cyr did, in 1900. Cyr had to get to the top of the cliffs, every day, to cut wood. He had a woodlot and a permit, and it was his woodlot that marked the first encroachment of the town into the wilderness on top of the cliffs. In an odd

reversal, what was an early site of human activity is
now one of the few places in the city where wilderness
can still be evoked.

Antoine and his brother Mike came up the Chilkoot
Pass and down the Yukon River in the rush of '98, two
of the many who stopped at Whitehorse, who saw the
chance to make a buck right then and there, rather than
grasp at the gold downriver that might never materialize. They were loggers, Acadian loggers from New
Brunswick, used to dancing on tree trunks in fast water.
In Whitehorse they became river pilots, navigating rafts
through Miles Canyon and the Whitehorse Rapids for
gold seekers on the fast track to Dawson City. When
the rush was over, Antoine and Mike started to deliver
wood and water to the growing town, and later they
managed the honey wagon as well.

I like to think of Antoine Cyr, driving his horse-drawn
wagon up his own road to the top of the cliffs. I like to
think of him working all day, all by himself in what was
then deep bush — alders and spruce and poplar,
according to the surveyors' maps of the time. Twenty
years later, Cyr's partially cleared woodlot became
Whitehorse's first airstrip, the precursor to today's
airport. It was much smaller then, and hastily cleared of
stumps and roots in preparation for the first planes
ever to land in the Yukon.

On August 16, 1920, four two-seater De Havilland
4Bs touched down on the plateau, and the whole town
came out to greet them. The First Alaska Air Expedition

had left Mineola, New York, on July 15 for a nine-thou-
sand-mile round-trip flight to Nome, Alaska, in order to
prove the viability of long-distance air travel. Whitehorse
was a pit stop along the way. When the planes arrived,
there were speeches and special presentations, and
that night there was a big ball. (The airmen couldn't
make it to the ball — they were due in Dawson — but
the citizens of Whitehorse were undeterred and
whooped it up without them.)

I like to imagine the scene, after the planes had
taken off: mothers and fathers and children and dogs
and dignitaries come down through the gulch, on foot,
in wagons, and even in cars — three or four citizens
owned cars, in those early days — all in their finery,
their feet sinking in the sand, their clothes covered in
dust. When they reached the bottom of the gulch, they
would still have to walk through the bush before they
reached town — there was nothing but bush northwest
of Strickland Street. When I'm up there on the cliffs
walking beside the Frost fence that encloses the airport, I like to imagine those tiny planes landing on a
bumpy field, a cleared patch in the bush, a scale that
was so much smaller and more intimate.

It was a favourite pastime, in Whitehorse's early
history, to take the air on a Sunday, to stroll up the Bridle
Path to the top of the cliffs, where rabbits and partridges
cavorted. The Bridle Path had two functions in the lives
and, more importantly, the psyches of the townspeople. It
represented a gracious urban walk, as found in cities

around the world, connecting the tiny northern town to larger civilization, at least in the imagination. At the same time, it connected the town to the larger wilderness that stood just outside its borders.

In late October of 1922, a young woman from New Zealand arrived in Whitehorse from Dawson City on the steamboat *Casca*, on the *Casca*'s last run of the season. Mary Davis and her sister, Nellie, had spent a month in Dawson being wined, dined, picnicked and danced off their feet by the entire town. Davis later wrote an account of her stay in the Yukon, which included a couple of months in Whitehorse, where once again she and her sister were the darlings of the social set. Soon after her arrival in Whitehorse, she was taken up the Bridle Path by one of her new friends. "From it we enjoyed a magnificent view of the town and were intrigued by the grouse and rabbits we saw along the way," she reports in the somewhat gushing tone of her journal.

I spent a good deal of time with Mary Davis (later Mary Davis Moody) recently, when I was researching a history of Whitehorse. I also spent a good deal of time walking along the base of the cliffs at Main Street and south to Lambert, trying to find the Bridle Path's point of origin. At the time, I was so involved in researching the 1920s that I didn't know that the Bridle Path had become a road in 1938, built by the White Pass and Yukon Route under contract to the federal Department of Transport. (Everybody just called it DOT in those

days.) It was a real road, paved and with guardrails.
Photographs taken in 1947 show that what is now a
wash of muck and mud in the spring and dry coarse
sand in the summer was a solid platform that sup-
ported army trucks and cars that came careering down
from the airport. Some evidence remains: a piece of
twisted guardrail, a thick wire cable springing out of the
ground. Erosion and landslides were a constant problem on that road — army bulldozers were on call to
clear the tons of clay and rubble that could descend
without warning after a rainfall. In 1948, the road was
closed entirely, much to the chagrin of Whitehorse
residents, who then had to go the long way to the
airport, up Two Mile Hill and around.

There is much confusion in my mind about the base
of the road that was the Bridle Path. A ramp of earth
stretches from the west end of T'eegatha O'zeah park
and peters out at the base of the steep part of the cliff.
But then, just behind the purple cabin at the head of
Lambert Street, another ramp of earth also extends
upward and disappears into the wall of the cliff. I
haven't found anyone who can tell me which is the
original path, and I'm not sure that I want to know. The
mysterious traces of an earlier Whitehorse both evoke
and satisfy the same kind of longing the clay cliffs do.
Both are associated with what is missing — either lost,
or impossible to find.

The plateau above the cliff, on the city side of the
airstrip, where today there are wild roses, lupines, and

even cranberries, and vast drifts of snow, used to be lined with buildings. Pan Am Airlines and CP Air had their hangars there, and the DOT buildings were beside them. It was only when erosion threatened the foundations in the late 1950s and early '60s that the buildings were moved to the far side of the airstrip, closer to the Alaska Highway. Once again, the remains are there — platforms of cracked cement with the occasional rusting bolt, just about where Main Street would intersect the cliff, if it continued all the way up.

Spectacular mudslides have occurred in the spring, when melting ice has de-stabilized the clay and turned it to liquid. For two or three weeks every spring, the cliffs are impossible to walk up or down, except in the early morning, when the mud is frozen. Once, in the early 1980s, a mudslide sheared a bedroom off one end of a house on Jarvis Street just as its owners were leaving for a movie. The instability of the clay in spring has been the subject of studies and special projects since the early 1950s. One federal employee, Robert F. Leggert, fell so much in love with the cliffs on his first trip to Whitehorse in 1953, that he came back in 1969 after he had retired, just to have a look at how they were doing. Had vegetation grown back on the section between Puckett's Gulch and Baxter's Gulch? (No, and it's the lack of vegetation and the deep clefts in the clay that give that section of cliff the look of buttes in Montana, or so I like to imagine on those days when I need to imagine myself somewhere else.) Had DOT kept its promise and moved its buildings to the other side of the airstrip? Yes, as we know. There is something infinitely appealing about this elderly civil servant coming back to check on a favourite spot, "this magnificent natural feature of the Yukon." The cliffs had got to him.

I know how he felt. The cliffs now have the same appeal for me that The End Of Broadway had in my childhood. Not really wilderness in themselves, they allow the projection of wilderness. They are ripe for fantasy. They take me somewhere else.

Another Fire

Dean Eyre

I'd call it a fortunate summer
that gave us two suns.
One
that circled above,
an eagle riding the gyre
of the solstice,
and the other
burning to powdery ash
the dead wood we culled
in ever widening circles,
giving light to light
and heat to uncooled earth.

And it was this other
that we circled.
We were its planets

and its votives.
We fed it
and it in its turn
gave us a centre
that could hold
so long
as the flames danced,
so long
as those fragrant days
of middle summer
refused to be caged
in branded calendars,

but summer is a leaky boat
and the waves it breasted in June
leave it almost awash in August.

I watched
a civilization rise
and explore its youth
in fits of love and energy.
We held each other
with fascination
in wonder at skin and muscle
so finely draped
about white shining bone.
We swam in water too cold
and danced on days too hot

and found that it was
all in all
enough.

Declining from this
through succeeding phases
of decadence
I observed our rituals
become more elaborate,
couches replaced stumps
and mattresses
let us rise
above the twisted floor,
and it took
more tequila to find harmony
than it had before
but the fire stayed the same
though the planets began to change
the nights grew colder
and one sun left us
and the other
that before had burned for joy
now burned for heat.

I left with a mystery
the day that the last
of the fireweed died
and returned without one

on a cold thanksgiving
determined to hold on to
everything I could remember.

Alone as a light snow fell
from a grey settling
twilight.
Before
the blackened pit:
a torn couch,
an engineless van,
and three great black bags of garbage
remained amongst the more
anonymous detritus,
and I felt
like an archaeologist
wandering my own people's ruins,
but as I stood,
where we'd all stood
at one time or another
to watch the flames flicker
on that patch of pounded earth,
there was
despite the snow
a faint flare of warmth
a single guitar note
and a gust of wind
that lifted soot
into the winter sky

The Gillis Library

Yvette Nolan

Atlinites are great readers. They read great books, by great authors (mostly dead), and pass those great books along to one another, so that they can discuss them at dinner parties. And if one of those great books by one of those late great authors should fall into your hands — say someone left it sitting on a chair at the Laundromat and Public Shower when his dryer stopped and he went to fold his clothes, and then in his haste to get his toasty well-faded Levi 501's and all-cotton Beefy-T's into his Landcruiser before the rain, he forgot it there on his chair — you might flip open the front cover to see if there were some inscription that would allow you to return that book to him, perhaps with a comment about his good taste in literature, or his domestic skills. And you might be surprised to find there, instead of "For my dearest son, love Mom" or "Marco, ich bin dein, Lilith," the stamp of The Gillis Library, Atlin.

You can walk up and down the streets of Atlin — First, Second, and Third — and you will never find The Gillis Library. The Liquor Store, the Red Cross Outpost, the Laundromat and Public Shower are all easy to find, but of The Gillis Library there is no sign. And yet, once you have discovered a loan from The Gillis Library, you begin to see borrowed books everywhere. The woman in front of you at James's store picking up two litres of milk and an eight-pack of toilet paper is carrying a hardcover biography of a dead author that looks suspiciously like a loaner from The Gillis Library. The guide and outfitter lying in his boat with his booted feet up on a pile of gear while he waits for his clients reads a mint-condition novel by an avant-garde (but dead) French writer, a novel that contains not a single "e," a novel that virtually screams The Gillis Library. When you walk into the Liquor Store to choose a nice Zinfandel for dinner, the woman behind the counter closes and puts to one side what you know must be a Gillis Library book.

"Oh, are you going up there?" she says when you show her the book you saved from the Laundromat and Public Shower. "Would you mind very much dropping off this one too?" and she reaches under the counter and hands you a very old, very grimy hardcover copy of *Moby Dick*. "I liked all the action bits, when they're hunting the whale and such," she says. "But all those endless chapters of exposition! This island and that painting and the sea, the sea, the sea! Where's the whale? I kept saying, get back to the whale!" She pauses and then winks. "But don't tell Himself that. I think it's his favourite book of all time."

When you follow her directions out of town, along the Warm Bay Road and take the turnoff she describes, you find yourself at The Gillis Library, only it isn't really a library, more of a room cobbled on as an afterthought to a cabin there in the woods. But what a room. Shelves and shelves and more shelves threaten to collapse under the weight of thousands of books, thick undeniable books, thin mere suggestions of books, paperbacks and hardcovers, brittle pages and mildewed pages, 25-cent second-hand books and cherished first editions, all very weighty.

The custodian of The Gillis Library is indeed The Gillis. He chuckles when you reverentially hand him the pale-covered grime-streaked water-spotted marbled Whale, and the pristine Samuel Johnson and tell him how you came into possession of those volumes and how you found your way to The Gillis Library.

"It's a joke," he says.

"I'm sorry?"

"Yeah. A joke. There is no Gillis Library, it's just my room. Someone once gave me one of those embossers. I think she was actually being sarcastic about how much time I spent with my books, but it turned out to be the most useful gift I have ever received. I spent three weeks embossing every book I own, and when I came out, she was gone. I suppose there's a lesson in there somewhere about sarcasm. Nicest parting gift she could have given me. She never came back, but you'd be surprised at how many books are returned because they have that stamp in them."

"Oh well, I'm — I just — wanted to — I thought you'd miss these books — " you stammer, inexplicably, disproportionately embarrassed by your perfectly reasonable assumption that this was a real library.

"Well, yeah, thanks, I really appreciate you coming all the way out here to bring them back. Say, do you want a cup of tea or something?"

Over peppermint tea, you tell him about how you just needed to get out of the city and you had stumbled on Atlin, happened to be in the Pine Tree when the waitress quit, how you had picked up the hamburger bun and the meat patty off the floor, piled the fries back on the plate, and been offered the job by Roger on the spot.

The custodian of The Gillis Library and the parting-gift-giver had come to Atlin as back-to-the-landers. They renounced the capitalist society, withdrew from urbania, and headed north to hew their own wood and fetch their own water, to grow and raise and harvest what they could, and to barter for what they couldn't. The gift-giver brought her paints and her tools for carving in stone. The custodian brought his books and his tools for building in wood. They built a series of cabins, the first a simple, one-room rectangle heated by a wood stove, the second a little more complex, a little better insulated and with electricity, since the power company now ran a line all the way out here anyway.

The third cabin had a second level — not a whole floor, mind you, just a loft for the sleeping space — and a hot tub, and water that came out of the taps, but only in the summer. And as the cabin became more and more — well, civilized, despite his intentions — the custodian began to spend more and more time with his books, until they threatened to overwhelm the whole space, until the gift-giver insisted that the custodian get rid of them all. So he built the room, the afterthought to this cabin, The Gillis Library that was nothing more than four walls of shelves with a window set in a wall of biographies.

In spite of the isolation, the books had multiplied. Once a year, before the gardening season began in earnest, the custodian of The Gillis Library made the trip to the Outside. He took with him two empty suitcases. After ten days, he returned with the two suitcases full of books, chosen from the second-hand shelves of Vancouver or Seattle or Winnipeg or Halifax. He was not even sure why he still collected them, these souvenirs of a life that he had renounced, relics of a world that no longer existed.

"More tea? I could put on the pot."

"Thank you, no, I should go."

"Say, if you're staying in Atlin for a while, you could borrow a book, you know," he tells you.

"Um, sure," you say, because the steady diet of two-day-old tabloids from the city and American celebrity rags has left you hungry for something more substantial, something that will sustain you through the long midnight sunlit night. "Do you have anyone — anyone — any living writers?"

He glowers at you, and for a moment you think you have offended him.

"Ah, how we can we know if they are any good if they aren't dead? Artists cannot be judged by their peers, only by history!"

"Oh — I — "

"Wait."

He disappears into the room and returns bearing a paperback, grey, new, the spine not even broken.

"Now *she's* good. Just won the Pulitzer for this poetry. Do you like poetry?"

"Yes," you say, "yes. She's not dead?"

"No, not dead. Polish."

You take the Polish poet's book and you thank The Gillis for the tea and the loan of the book, and you get in your rusty Hyundai and manoeuvre down the driveway. Within seconds, the cabin, the custodian, and The Gillis Library are gone from view, but from the seat beside you, the Polish poet's paperback sings with promise.